D0306589

In Place of Failure

Making It Yes Next Time ... Soon

Vagabond Voices
Glasgow

© Jim Sillars 2015

First published in September 2015 by
Vagabond Voices Publishing Ltd.,
Glasgow,
Scotland.

ISBN 978-1-908251-51-0

The author's right to be identified as author of this book under
the Copyright, Designs and Patents Act 1988 has been asserted.

Cover design by Mark Mechan

Typeset by Park Productions

For further information on Vagabond Voices, see the website,
www.vagabondvoices.co.uk

In Memory of Councillor Jim Mitchell of Paisley without whom and others like him slogging through the difficult years, the SNP would not have survived to reach the heights it has done in recent years, and my thanks to the Margo Mobile team: Gil, Iain, Peter, Calum, Heather, Frank, Jonathon and Mhairi

Foreword

In Part I, I attempt to set out the claims made by Better Together against independence, identify why the Yes side did not successfully contest and rebut a number of them, and put forward answers that may help the independence movement prepare better, and be more effective, next time. In Part II, I address some issues that do not necessarily concern the referendum now past, but may be of relevance next time.

The fact is that Yes lost, and there are reasons why we lost. The huge surge in membership of the SNP, and the smashing victory it obtained in the Westminster 2015 elections, and the pleasure it has given Yes voters, have meant that there has been little attempt to examine why we lost.

This book is a personal view on the reasons for the result. Hopefully there have already been, or will be, others with different views. It is important that as many of us as possible look at what happened during the campaign and for the reason it culminated in defeat on polling day.

We do not all need to agree, but a wide-ranging critical examination of how Yes dealt with the issues and challenges flung at us will make us better prepared next time, both in respect of policies and organisation.

In a BBC *Question Time* in January 2014, the panel

was asked what would happen if Scotland voted No. I replied that by 2016 many of those who voted No would bitterly regret it. I did so in the knowledge of the extension of austerity that would come after the Westminster election in 2015, which would hit all classes except the rich, and that Scots would then see that the only way out would be independence.

I would prefer that austerity did not continue, that the pain and poverty it brings did not happen, but there is no escaping the reality of austerity and the damage it does to individuals and communities. That makes escape from the UK imperative. I hope that day of departure will be soon.

Jim Sillars, Edinburgh, September 2015

Introduction

"Out of self-respect comes self-confidence, and out of that comes imagination, innovation, and the whole world opens up to us with independence."
— Margo MacDonald

Compare that inspired message with its vision of new horizons, new opportunities, of breaking free from old narrow boundaries that constrict the mind, with the present state of the Scots – back now where we have always been, paying the price of failure, *spending energy in protest, bereft of the power to use it in rebuilding our nation.*

All my life Scottish workers have been forced to engage in protest movements. Against unemployment, closures and more unemployment, deindustrialisation, erosion of trade union rights, bad housing, the poll tax, welfare cuts, Trident, and austerity. Once again we are on the defensive.

With the referendum lost, the energy this nation could be using for positive purposes, to create a new economic model and improve our society, is now employed in protests against what is happening as another dose of austerity is administered by a government that, not only did we not vote for, but one we comprehensively rejected.

If we are to move from the dismal situation that the pro-tests arise from, then independence isn't a dream that will never die; it is something that we must make a reality as soon as possible, and not in a generation from now.

On 18 September 2014 the referendum was lost, but not Scottish independence. The idea of a one-off never to be repeated for thirty years (the definition of generation in the dictionary) was an illusion held by the Unionists. While they were prepared to rubbish every statement made by Alex Salmond, they grasped at the one he made about a generation between refer-enda. There was no single leader of the Yes campaign. Alex spoke for his government, but had no authority to commit the rest of Yes to that timetable. Alex, like everyone else, is entitled to change his mind on this, as "events" take place in the most unexpected ways, and if the tenor of his remarks in 2015 is a guide, he may be reconsidering. Many hope so.

There can be no let-up on the struggle for independ-ence. To that end we need to look at the issues that stood out in the referendum, and deal with them. It is time to learn the lessons of that first attempt, inject ideas into the movement, in order that Yes succeeds next time, and ensure that next time is soon.

The victorious Unionists were affronted that the defeated Yes side did not creep away into a corner, weep and accept the verdict. They thought Alex Salmond's "a dream that will never die" a piece of empty rhetoric, not understanding that he was articulating the spirit of forces unleashed in Scotland by the referendum expe-rience. People do not want independence as an end in itself, but as a means to a new Scotland where the idea of social justice will permeate every public policy and our economic activity. For 45% of Scots, the United Kingdom and the traditional hold it had over us came to an end in the referendum. That task now is to make the 45 a majority.

Although parts of this book look at reasons for the defeat, where the Yes side was at its weakest and how we replace that with strength, this is not a blame game. Everyone who took part in the Yes campaign did so out of conviction, and with an energy and commitment not seen in Scottish political life before. However, a campaign that did not succeed must be critically examined, with areas identified where the Unionist Project Fear was able to sow uncertainty, and also where the defect as well as the strength of the Yes diversity played its part. Such an examination is essential to ensure that the next referendum is the last one we need to fight.

We now have had the experience of everything that Unionists can throw against independence. Everything is the right word. Lies, deceit, coercion of employees, false promises, threats to pensioners, foreign intervention, it was all put into play. Now we know. Next time we must make sure we are prepared.

I hope this book will be a contribution to the examination of the referendum and the thinking that must be done now, before the elections to the Scottish Parliament in 2016.

Nicola Sturgeon, during the Westminster election, said the timing of the next move to independence through a referendum is a matter for the Scottish people. But of course they can only decide on that if a political party seeks a mandate for independence and a referendum in an election. We shall have to wait and see which political parties seek seats in the Scottish

Parliament next year with that mandate up front in the manifestos.

The Unionist anxiety about another early referendum is instructive. They are terrified at the prospect, because the sooner it happens the less effective another Project Fear will be, and they know that the election of a Tory government, likely to be repeated in 2020 due to boundary redistribution in England, combined with more austerity cuts, is likely to stretch Scottish patience to breaking point.

It is no secret that I would like to see the SNP Holyrood manifesto ask the Scots to give the party a mandate for independence, and a referendum at a time of our choosing over the next four years. The election to Holyrood of a party and/or parties with an independence mandate should be the start of a major public campaign to get support up from 45% to 60%, and when that is accomplished, as it can be, that is the time for the referendum. I hope this book will contribute to that objective.

PART I

The No strategy in 1979
Project Fear

Unionist scaremongering in the 2014 referendum worked on sections of the electorate, especially but not exclusively on the elderly. It was a tried-and-tested tactic, exactly the same as proved so successful for No in the 1979 referendum for a Scottish Assembly.

Many, particularly young people, will be unfamiliar with the history. It is this: Labour promised a Scottish Assembly that, to quote the slogan then used, would create a "Powerhouse Scotland". The reality was that the Assembly on offer had very little power, but despite that Labour MPs led by George Cunningham, a Scot sitting for a London seat, inserted a rule in the Act that Yes had to get 40% of the total electorate; that meant anyone who did not vote, or names on the register not able or entitled to vote, like the dead, counted for the No side. The referendum was fought on an old electoral register so there were lots of dead and lots of errors. Yes won with 51.62%, but that was only 32.9% of the total register, not enough to leap the 40% barrier, and so no Assembly. We got Margaret Thatcher instead.

The 1979 campaign was a nightmare. Every newspaper, except the *Scotsman* under Eric Mackay's editorship, and the rest of the media was for No. A large number of Labour MPs campaigned for No. There was no money on the Yes side, while No was backed by the rich and big business. Social media didn't exist then to combat the official media. There was no single Yes campaign. Yes was split organisationally.

The No side ran an unashamed fear campaign. Business would up sticks and depart if we voted Yes. Jobs would be lost everywhere: steel jobs, mining jobs, banking jobs would all go. One woman I met in New Cumnock said she was voting No because her son worked in Customs and Excise on our west coast and would lose his job. I could not persuade her that an Assembly had very little power, and that Customs continued to be a UK responsibility. She was so terrified she was unable to take in what I was saying, because the whole No campaign was about the dreadful things that would happen with devolution.

On one famous occasion, to emphasise just how profoundly Scotland would be separated from England because of the Assembly, the No side put people on a Kings Cross to Edinburgh train. When it passed Berwick, they put on uniforms and went round demanding to see the passengers' passports.

The Better Together strategy in 2014 Project Fear

In 2014 Labour MPs sowed fear among the workers involved in warship building on the Clyde, saying there would be no more orders if Yes won. Talk about déjà vu: I recall standing at the gates of Govan Shipbuilders in 1979 listening to George Cunningham, up from London, telling the men that if they voted Yes, there would be no more warships built in Scotland. I watched those big men of the Clyde put their heads down, shuffle their feet, and exhibit fear. At that time there were around 25,000 shipbuilding jobs, so the fear he sowed spread. Today there are only around 3,000 shipbuilding jobs, no steel ones and no mining ones either.

We on the Yes side were ill-equipped to combat Project Fear in 1979. The 2014 Yes campaign was different. It had money, social media and thousands working in local Yes campaigns. We were in a much better position than 1979. Yet, the Fear still worked to a far greater extent than it should have. The No side worked to create uncertainty and fear. Uncertainty is not by itself fear, but it paves the way to its exploitation, while naked fear was let loose on the pensioners.

Perhaps because so few of us involved in the 1979 campaign were still politically active, we were not asked about our experience, and so the 2014 campaigners had no history to draw on to understand what was to be unleashed upon them, and so were not as prepared as they should have been.

That long gap between 1979 and 2014, thirty-five years, when new generations were born and unaware of the past tactics, helped make Project Fear effective. There will be no such gap when we engage in the next independence referendum. We know what is coming, and will be able to combat it.

Better Together Claim No. 1: The Most Successful Union Ever Scotland in the UK, Historical Context

The drive to Scottish independence, the uncoupling of our country from England, is not an accident, or due only to the mismanagement of the Scottish economy. The need for Scotland to be distinct, to exercise control over itself, is as long as the Union itself. Indeed, the Act of Union gave birth to a desire for home rule, which has been evident in Scottish politics for centuries.

However, that home rule desire was always couched within the Union, and the reason for it being so was the Empire, about which the Scottish aristocracy, and the middle and upper middle classes were enthusiasts in its extension, and from which they gained substantially. Those gains came from the slave trade, and also from its products, cotton from the southern United States, sugar and tobacco from the West Indies. The Scots Jardine and Matheson, operating out of Hong Kong, saw their illegal opium business in China flourish, and when threatened by the Chinese government they could and did call on the Empire's military might to ensure, through the Opium Wars, that their trade was protected. In 1880, 6,500 tonnes of opium were smuggled into China. Drug running on a massive scale, one of the successes of the Union? The Chinese see it differently.

In addition to business opportunities, the management of the Empire and the rewards it offered, especially in India, were often in the hands of Scots, including the officer ranks in the army of the East India Company, and then of the British military when the government in London took over full control following the 1875 Mutiny.

So, it has been a successful Union for some, albeit a minority, in Scotland and England. What about the majority? No doubt, when extolling the virtues of a three-hundred-year Union, Unionists will insist upon taking into account the shipbuilding on the Clyde where Scots workers contributed towards the creation of the largest merchant marine ever seen, and jobs in the coal and steel industries which supported shipbuilding. Unlike the benefits gained by the upper classes, workers had a different experience in the Empire, yet it cast its spell even on them. Scots workers were as enthusiastic and jingoistic for the Empire as others in the UK.

I recall as a primary school child, as late as the 1940s, sitting under a huge wall map with parts of the world painted red, and being told they belonged to "us". Most of us in that class were from hard up families, yet somehow felt as though we had a proprietorial stake in that map. It was "ours". I served in the Royal Navy between 1950 and 1960; not only on the patriotic mess decks was there strong opposition to decolonisation, but among the general population also. That map painted red cast a very wide spell.

The history of the Empire and Union for the majority was poverty, low wages, unemployment, slum housing, children with rickets, oppression of trade unions, and periods of unemployment. In 1862, of children born in Glasgow, 50% died before the age of five years. In 1897 22% of Scottish families lived in a one roomed house; in Glasgow it was 33%. In 1882, the Duke of Argyll, who owned all the houses in Inverary, threw out the Medical Officer of Health who had dared to report adversely on the sanitary state of the burgh after an outbreak of smallpox. In 1903, a Royal Commission found that 70% of schoolchildren in four Edinburgh schools were defective in some way. (History of the Scottish Working Classes in Scotland, by Tom Johnstone)

Here is a description of an area of Birmingham in 1910 by Field Marshall Slim, who was a teacher there: "Rats were endemic, toilet facilities primitive, diets inadequate, hygiene impossible, rickets and typhoid were common" (Uncle Bill: the Authorised Biography of Field Marshall Viscount Slim, by Russell Millar). There was the famous occasion in the 1930s, in my home county of Ayrshire, at a county council meeting, when Clarice McNab Shaw, a Labour councillor and later MP for Kilmarnock, stood with the tears coursing down her cheeks as the Tory administration rejected her motion to supply milk to children to prevent rickets.

There was, of course, one "glorious" option always available to young Scotsmen and others: to join the British army, fight to extend and maintain the Empire, and die for it. Scottish regimental battle honours show this was the case. On the whole, not something to celebrate.

The UK is a fiction

J.K. Rowling seems to think that when I describe the political relationship between Scotland and England, and note the dominance of the latter, she has evidence of an anti-English attitude. The problem is in her mind, not mine.

Reading memoirs and reports from those who managed the UK and its policies until very recent times, it was usually referred to as England. Even when Scots were involved at its highest levels, Lord Dalhousie for example as Governor General in India, they were found to be talking about how developments within the Empire affected England. That mindset set the policies.

The United Kingdom is a fiction. It is England with Scottish, Welsh and north of Ireland appendages. When Disraeli, in the House of Commons, 163 years after the Union, spelt out the consequences of Bismarck creating a united Germany, he said that the one country to be threatened by it was England. It was no different when Winston Churchill (former MP for Dundee) wrote his six-volume memoir of the Second World War in 1948: 241 years after the Union, he spoke the same language to describe what we were always led to believe was the UK.

Here are only a few excerpts from Churchill, from many similar throughout those volumes:

Referring to the growing concern about Germany in 1938: "At this time there was a great drawing together of men and women of all parties in England who saw the perils of the future" (Vol. 1, p. 195).

Referring to a radio broadcast by the then Prime Minister Neville Chamberlain on 27 September 1938: "While the Fuehrer was at grips with his generals, Mr. Chamberlain himself was preparing to broadcast to the English nation" (Vol. 1, p. 283).

There was the famous debate in the House of Commons on 2 September 1938, with Chamberlain under pressure for appeasement. As Arthur Greenwood rose to speak for Labour "Mr. Amery from the Conservative benches cried out to him 'Speak for England'" (Vol. 1, p. 362).

Mr. Churchill as prime minister, in a war in which Scots made up a good part of the British armed forces, made the following official minute to the Foreign

Secretary on 9 July 1941: "We propose replying to the agent for Pétain and Huntziger to the effect that: England has no interest in Syria except to win the war" (Vol. III, p. 714).

Even today the mask often slips. Tim Shipman, political editor of the *Sunday Times*, 7 June 2015, tells us that: "The English government's referendum bill is due to receive its second reading … on Tuesday."

1707 and all that

Two sovereign states joined together in 1707 to create a new state. That happened formally in legal terms, but in political terms and in terms of power and interests, it never happened. The English Parliament did not dissolve. It was, as the speaker at the time ruled, the English Parliament continuing, with some extra members drawn from Scotland. The rules and procedures of the English Parliament remained in force.

Before any reader thinks that what I am about to write is an anti-English tract, railing against the English statesmen of the eighteenth century, who trapped Scotland, let me disabuse you. Had the circumstances been the same, but the positions reversed, with a large richer Scotland concerned about its southern border, and a smaller poorer England, the Scots at that time would have done exactly the same as the English, and for the same reasons of security and foreign policy.

There are people in Scotland, in past generations and now, who are resentful about how Scotland was manipulated into the Union. I am not. There is no point in that position. What we have to understand and deal with are the consequences of Scottish-English realpolitik, which is that of the larger component dominating the smaller.

There never could be a merging of the two kingdoms into one genuine new entity. A large rich state does not dissolve itself in a partnership with a much smaller poor one: it absorbs the tiddler, whatever the legal window dressing may say. This was not a constitutional marriage of equals. Scotland was poor and ripe for plucking by an English state which needed to lock up its northern border so that there could be no more French threat from that direction.

The capture of Scotland was a triumph for English foreign policy, and a salutary lesson in the use of power. A weak economic Scotland post-Darien was wide open for economic and political attack, and it came in the form of the English Alien Act 1705, which was a response to the Scottish Act of Security 1704, which in turn was a response to the English Act of Settlement 1701, determining the monarchical succession. Scots, whose monarch was shared with England, were not prepared with the 1704 Act to accept willy-nilly the English view on this matter, especially as they had not been consulted.

The English 1705 Act was designed to force Scotland into a Union through intense economic pressure. A sanctions regime. It was made clear that unless Scotland started to negotiate a Union, Scottish trade with England would be prohibited in goods that mattered, and Scots would have no protection in English law for any property they may had in that country. Against that a Union would guarantee a free trade area, and Scottish access to the growing markets of the new Empire emerging. It was and could only be no contest.

England gave nothing away. The Kingdom of England was and remains the largest part of this supposed new entity, and so its interests above all will always be those expressed and pursued. When Ted Heath negotiated EEC entry in 1972, Scotland's fisheries became his throwaway card, despite it being of particular economic importance in our economy. This unequal partnership, and how it has been portrayed internationally, as England, has lain at the heart of much of Scottish nationalism. It is also the reason why, until very recent times, the English did not need to define themselves by nationality. For them, England was Britain and British was English.

For over three hundred years Scots have often taken refuge in the illusion that we are equal partners in this Union, whereas the reality has always been as the English mindset saw it, their country as the superior partner, whose national interests come first. That "English" mindset is not anti-Scottish, either deliberately or unconsciously, it is built on the reality of what actually happened in 1707, and the years following it.

The end of empire

England, with a significant contribution from Scots, built an empire that ranks in comparison with any other, including that of Rome. Whatever justifications are made for empires, such as extending civilisation and, as was said frequently when I was young, taking on the "white man's burden", they are created by naked power for the purposes of creating captive markets and the plunder of wealth. There is a frieze in a room in the Foreign Office showing Britannia sitting on her throne with India and the other colonies pouring their wealth at her feet. There were no guilty hang-ups in those days. Exploitation was the order of the day.

The necessary subjugation of other peoples in building an empire, and the moral questions that arise from the expropriation of their wealth that empire entailed, are not the subject of this book. In passing, however, it has to be noted that the colonial people conquered, racially insulted, exploited and robbed are unlikely to have seen this Union and the empire it built, as a success.

The point to be grasped now is that we are in a post-empire era, with what remains at the centre a shadow of a once mighty economic power. When Unionists tell us that Scotland must remain part of the UK in order to be supported by its strength, they may believe it but delude themselves. The UK has no inherent strength with which to throw a protective economic blanket over Scotland. David Torrance, the *Herald* (2 March 2015), claimed that some supporters of independence describe the UK as a "failed state". It is not that, but it is struggling with the inevitable weakness that affects all empires as they move into the final stage of imperial decline.

Take a careful look at the UK behind the propaganda and self-delusion level. It is in crisis, but most of the people don't know it. With one exception, the monarchy, all the pillars that hold up that state are eroding in that terminal decline. Parliament is no longer a revered institution. The Church of England is split on doctrine, weak, and of little relevance to national life. Its justice system, with its record of covering up for abusers, is rotten to its establishment core. The armed forces have been hollowed out. Its economy cannot pay its way, and is dangerously imbalanced due to over-reliance on financial services which are, themselves, relying on external actors remaining happy with its casino banking. It is kept afloat on an ocean of debt – £1.5 trillion national debt and £1.474 trillion of private debt – and debt off the books with PFIs of an additional £222 billion, much of which Gordon Brown is responsible for.

The growth in the economy, boasted of by the Tories during the 2015 election, was due entirely to extra consumer demand built upon further individual and household debt. £100 million was the increase in total net lending to individuals in one month, March 2015. The ocean of debt gets bigger and deeper.

Far from being embraced by the strength of the British state, Scotland's chance of building a new economy able to deliver growth, quality jobs, high wages and a fair society is being suffocated because we are locked into a state in irreversible decline.

As others see it

People within the boundaries of the UK, living day to day, are unlikely to see that stark picture of decline, especially as it is rarely something openly discussed. Unionist politicians punt an opposite picture to the reality, using words, as Cameron did during the Westminster election, about the UK being "great". The avoidance of debate around the debt and its cause was lamented in the financial pages of newspapers during the election, but they are read only by a minority.

In other pages of the newspapers reality was ignored. In the run-up to the election last May, in an effort to promote defence expenditure as an issue, columnists wrote in terms of the UK's need to remain a "world power". The imperial mind tends to outlive the empire.

The final stages of decline are seen at their clearest by people outside of the UK. Here is Stryker McGuire, an Anglophile, contributing a view of the UK in *Newsweek* away back on 1 August 2009:

> Forget the Great in Britain – its fall was inevitable, but the economic crisis will shrink the last pretences of empire faster than anyone expected.
>
> Even in the decades after losing its empire, Britain strode the world like a pocket superpower. Its economic strength and cultural heft, its nuclear-backed military might, its extraordinary relationship with America – all these things helped this small island nation to punch well above its weight class. ... Now all that is changing ... . Suddenly ... the country is having to rethink its role in the world – perhaps as Little Britain, certainly as a lesser Britain. ... History has been closing in on Britain for some time.

The Yes campaign organisation; strengths, weaknesses and the role of the SNP

The Yes Scotland's central organisation in Glasgow was seen as too close to the SNP in the formative stages of the campaign, perhaps not surprising as the party provided its start-up costs, and it never quite shook off the Better Together gibe about it being an SNP front. Its advisory board was just that, not an executive board, and that was a mistake, as will be seen when I come to deal with currency. Before the vote, the SNP paid Yes Scotland £275,000 towards its campaign costs, and subsequent to the vote paid over £550,000 in order that it could meet its bills.

It is not a criticism of the SNP to say they partly funded Yes Scotland, or stood behind it in those final days of the campaign when so much was at stake. Nor is it a criticism of Yes Scotland that it took the money. If the SNP had not continued to contribute, and or had Yes Scotland refused, the campaign would have been badly damaged.

What we have to look at, as a lesson for next time, is the structural and organisational weaknesses that led to Yes Scotland having to rely so heavily on one political party.

How was it formed? Who were the original architects of Yes Scotland was never clear. How the chief executive was chosen, how the advisory board was chosen, what the respective remits were and who set them out? Who was the guiding hand or hands, is the question.

It was one that intrigued our household, because in its early stages of formation the chief executive visited Margo MacDonald at our home to arrange for her to be vice-chair to Dennis Canavan in the chair. Before 9 a.m. a day or two later, again at home, she had a telephone conversation with someone handling the PR to agree to the statement she would make as vice-chair. Ten minutes later she was phoned by the chief executive to be told that she was not to be the vice-chair. For the sake of unity, Margo made no protest either privately or in public. This is the first time this episode has been made known.

Margo at that time was able to take part in planning and campaigning. That someone of her stature, experience and drawing power with the public should be chosen and then unchosen, and by a person unknown, is an indication that there was something not right about how Yes Scotland was put together.

The Yes campaign had strength in depth, yet it also had that salient weakness of an SNP connection. The latter will have to be addressed and removed for next time. That will not be easy. It will require wisdom, and willingness to cooperate on the part of all who will be engaged, especially the membership and parliamentary leadership of the SNP.

The strength in depth came from the number of local Yes groups, in which thousands of people right across the political spectrum came together, learnt organisation, and engaged in political study and action. Rarely did those local groups rely on one political party, the SNP. But in the national campaign, as covered by the media, the role of SNP and its leadership eclipsed the rest, and that proved a weakness.

We had a national effort based on local activists, while the national case for independence was seen mainly as devolving on the SNP and its government White Paper. Women for Independence, the National Collective, Business for Scotland, the Scottish Socialist Party, the Scottish Green Party, Labour for Independence, Academics for Yes, and others all were engaged and energised the campaign ... but the Unionist media and Unionist parties sought, and succeeded, in focusing the public on the SNP and the White Paper.

Time after time on Yes platforms a speaker would start by saying, "This is not about Alex Salmond and the White Paper." That betrayed a weakness. Indeed this was driven home in the STV debate between Alex Salmond and Alistair Darling, when Bernard Ponsonby asked Darling if he would admit to Alex having a mandate for his White Paper if there was a Yes vote. Darling spotted the opportunity, and quickly said yes, thus pinning the referendum to the White Paper. He was not contradicted by Alex.

This weakness has to be examined free of rancour and blame. But questions have to be asked, and answered. Was the White Paper an SNP party document, or was it a production solely from the SNP Scottish government? There is a difference. Obviously it came from the government. That leads on to the question of whether that government canvassed opinions from its backbenchers, from the Advisory Board of Yes Scotland and others before it was published.

There is no evidence of an input to the White Paper from anyone outside the Scottish government and its Fiscal Commission. I recall waiting in line for Margo's copy. Next to me was an SNP MSP. I said to him, "You know the difference between you and me? It isn't that you are an MSP. When we pick up that White Paper, I am not bound by it, I can disagree with it, but you are already bound to every word, even though standing here you have not a clue as to what it says." He did not contradict me.

That White Paper, drawn up by a very small group of people, compromised the wider Yes movement on two key issues – a currency union and the 10% reduction in corporation tax. It seemed evident to me that a currency union was a gift to the Unionists and that the corporation tax cut was a gift to the Labour Party. Those of us who saw these flaws could do nothing about the 10%, but as the Fiscal Commission had laid out choices on currency, I lobbied hard for a Plan B. In one email exchange with Crawford Beveridge, chair of the Fiscal Commission, dated 27 February 2014, I wrote bluntly: "The Commission and Alex have led us into a trap, and the quicker this is understood the better." Crawford was kind enough to meet me on 5 March 2014 in the Scottish Parliament where he had earlier been giving evidence on the currency issue. I had asked to meet the Fiscal Commission but that did not prove possible, so I handed him the following note, asking him to make its contents known to other members of the Commission:

The Commission chose a currency union as the best option for an independent Scotland. Leaving aside the transfer of sovereignty involved in that policy, the Commission assumed that both Scottish and Westminster governments would settle down to pre-referendum talks, and that both would agree on the detailed arrangements required to make it work once a Yes vote became the new reality. That was naive – a total discounting of political reality.

The Commission posited a role for the Scottish government in the make-up of the macroeconomic policy to be agreed in the new sterling zone, and the construction of a new Monetary Policy Committee of the Bank of England. Here again was an assumption of not only cooperation, but a willingness on the part of the government in London to accommodate the Commission's recommendations, all of which required surrender of sovereignty by rUK, and a root and branch reconstruction of its machinery.

These assumptions were, at root, political. There was no consideration that in the political sphere, this side of 18 September, the sterling zone would be rejected by the present Coalition government, and its possible successors. A rejection was predictable, and there were those of us who predicted it.

The result now is that there is no currency plan. The rejection by Osborne, Balls and Alexander removes a currency union, and as there has been no chosen alternative, the SNP government is left arguing that rUK will change its mind post-Yes. As that cannot be proved, the contention of there being no currency plan remains true.

But let us suppose that rUK does change its attitude. Therein lies the trap that a one-club currency policy has created. rUK holds all the aces. The Scottish government, with no Plan B, has to approach London as a supplicant. rUK sets the rules of the currency union, and Scotland is in the position of take it or leave it. There is, then, no alternative but to take what is on offer – and without a doubt what will be on offer will be entirely to London's advantage.

The political position today, as I have discovered from listening to people at the many meetings I have spoken at, is that the Yes side in this campaign is now dangerously weak without a Plan B.

I am aware that the Commission is linked to the Scottish government, but it has a wider responsibility to the people of Scotland, and the exercise of that independent responsibility is now needed. If the Scottish government will not get itself out of the corner it painted itself into, then you and the Commission will have to do it. You cannot claim that you are mere technicians, highly skilled ones, with no political role. As I wrote above, your assumptions took you into the realm of politics, and it is incumbent upon the Commission to start fixing the political mess that much of the Yes side are in – that is those who follow the SNP line.

You will be aware that there are many of us who do not follow that line. We do not, however, carry the weight given to the Commission by the media. We shall try to rectify that, but our efforts should not be necessary if the Commission now did the job needed.

There were signs of movement, with Crawford

Beveridge examining the currency union and possible alternatives in a lecture at Glasgow Caledonian University – and it was obvious in the second BBC Salmond-Darling debate that Alex had done work on alternatives. But what was required did not happen, that is the formal abandonment of the currency union, and a clear commitment to and explanation of the benefits of a separate Scottish pound. Without that, the uncertainty was not removed.

I also got in touch with some members of the Yes Scotland Advisory Board to persuade them that, whatever the SNP government said about a currency union, the broad campaign had to have a Plan B, our own currency.

At one meeting of the Advisory Board, there was a majority for an alternative Plan B, but that majority was persuaded that to declare for a Plan B would be seen as the Yes side being split. Common sense gave way to the imperative of supporting the White Paper, and thus of lining up the central organisation with the SNP. So, the whole Yes movement found itself tied to an SNP policy which many, very many, did not agree with. A policy that was damaging. Disclaimers on platforms that we were not voting for the White Paper could not overcome that. Why the currency union was a mistake is dealt with later in this book.

Could the White Paper have been different? It can be argued from the purist position that a government White Paper, which is after all government policy, and paid for by the taxpayer, must at the end of any process come from within government. But that White Paper was no normal document; it stood at the centre of debate, taken by a hostile media as the main reference point of guidance to the future with independence. Moreover, it was evident that SNP ministers expected support for it from various groups and people who had no association with the SNP as a party, and whose opinion has not been asked.

Like many of those others, I could not support the White Paper in its entirety, despite being a member of the party. It was a hybrid – a statement of facts and information, but combined with an SNP election manifesto in the event of a Yes majority. What leapt from its pages was an SNP programme for "change no change", whereas most of the groups campaigning Yes wanted radical change.

Once independent, Scotland's wide diversity of views will be subject to judgement at an election; therefore there is nothing wrong with different views being presented during a referendum about the Scotland people seek. But to have one dominant publication from a government written in such a way as to give the clear impression that its view would prevail was a structural fault.

Getting it right next time
Need action now

Organisation & Funds. It is not sensible to wait until we approach the next referendum before acting. Action is necessary *now*, so that any central Yes Scotland is not reliant on any one political party for start-up funding or running costs. It should be possible *now, to set up a Yes Referendum Trust Fund,* with trustees drawn from the various organisations still in existence, and build it up through crowdfunding and other fundraising.

There are 1,600,000 people who voted Yes. We should be able to raise funds from that base, with a well-organised, professional fundraising operation that would combine with meetings and discussion groups to keep the Yes activists engaged, and the movement alive and ready for the next time.

Remit. The trustees could take on the job of setting out the structures and remit for the central organisation. I would suggest one function, research, as being a priority.

The SNP. Yes will require the SNP and other parties to seek and win a mandate for independence. It is probable that in such a circumstance, we shall again have an SNP government, either with a majority or able to muster a majority in concert with other parties.

However important the SNP is to the future of independence, we cannot again have a government White Paper which, whether intended or not, subsumes other views that are equally valid.

The SNP government's contribution should be restricted to the production of a factual document explaining the contribution each sector of the economy makes to GDP and GNP, the balance between manufacturing and services, the banks and financial institutions' share of services, a description of North Sea oil and gas, field by field, the number of rigs at work, the size of the offshore and onshore workforces, income and other taxes, and what is drawn from each component of the economy, the number of small businesses and their workforces, numbers employed in the public sector, numbers employed in the private sector, the cost of government services, Scottish contribution to the likes of HS2 and major capital works on London transport, foreign office expenditure, defence expenditure, and the share of UK real estate that would fall to an independent Scotland, and the rights of state pensioners and those in company pension funds.

The SNP as a party, note as a party, will be as free as any other Yes group to state and publish its view of the future, but it should not carry the imprimatur of "government," and would thus not be the dominant voice against which all else was judged.

In addition, to give cohesion to the national Yes campaign, there should be published a document of agreed principles from all the campaigning groups: the length of the transitional period to independence, how a negotiating team and its backup should be formed, the date of the first independence elections, the method of election, how a convention will be formed to write a draft constitution, that the ECHR would stand central to that constitution, that a referendum be held on the monarchy. Agreement on currency must be set out in this document.

Better Together Claim No. 2: No one knows the currency we shall use

I and others erred in believing that when Alex Salmond wiped the floor with Alistair Darling in the second BBC debate, the currency issue had been put aside. We should have known better. Better Together knew better, and kept on and on about the uncertainty surrounding what currency would be used. Postreferendum research by Edinburgh University showed that currency was a potent factor right up to and on polling day, and not to the advantage of Yes.

The choice made by the SNP government, a currency union with England, had technical and economic merit. Alex Salmond, with the Fiscal Commission's work to aid him, was correct in saying it was as much in rUK's interest to have one as it was in Scotland's. The English economy imports more than it exports, and has a huge balance of trade deficit. Scotland on the other hand has a balance of trade surplus, a large one. If what Scotland contributes to the UK trade balance is taken away, then the weakness of the rUK economy would be laid bare, with consequent pressure on the pound sterling.

Those technical economic arguments left out the most vital factor of all – the politics. It would have taken two to agree a currency union. If one said no, there could not be one. It was obvious that the UK chancellor, along with Labour and Lib Dems, would say No. In doing so they created what the No side needed, uncertainty. I had thought when Osborne flew north for his few hours to say No, that the SNP government would see that it was off the hook. That Osborne No allowed it to say, "If you don't want something that is obviously beneficial to your country and business, if you want to cut off your nose to spite our face, then so be it, we have an alternative suitable for us and us alone – our own currency which we shall link one-to-one with sterling, something you can do nothing to prevent." It would seem that such an opportunity was not considered.

Constant repetition by the SNP government that the pound sterling was as much ours as it was Westminster's did nothing to remove the uncertainty. It was an argument many Scots accepted, but it was a specious one. In fact, the pound sterling is only ours because we are part of the British state. Leave the British state and it is not ours. Without a currency union sterling would be a foreign currency, the sole issuing authority being the Bank of England, an institution of what remained of the British state. Whether it continued to be called the UK or not, that state would own sterling and Scotland wouldn't.

I have no doubt that had there been a Yes majority, the UK Treasury would have rapidly changed its tune. But throughout the campaign, and as a major contributor to uncertainty, the proposal of a currency union was a gift to the No side.

Better with our own pound

As well as the political lesson learnt, there are other sound reasons, economic ones, for rejecting a currency union. A currency union means a monetary union, which must in turn impinge upon fiscal policy, which in turn reduces independence, as the southern states in the Eurozone have discovered. Moreover, a currency union between five million people and fifty-five million, with the fifty-five million providing through the Bank of England a lender of last resort, would be dangerously imbalanced. Given that there was no Plan B, our negotiating position in settling the currency union agreement would have been very weak, because the other side would have known we had nowhere else to go. If they let us in, it would be on their terms.

There would have been no chance of the rUK Chancellor of the Exchequer giving up his right to nominate the governor of the bank, or the four outside members of the Monetary Policy Committee. The MPC has five members drawn from within the bank, plus those four. How many would Scotland get? One, maybe two. Their influence would have been negligible.

The only conclusion we can reach from that scarring experience, is no more talk of currency union. The independence movement must opt for the most obvious and sensible alternative, our own currency.

It is the exchange value that counts

Exchange value between a Scottish pound and sterling is what is important for Scottish business trading with our major markets in England, Wales and Northern Ireland. That is particularly so for our financial sector as the bulk of its trade and transactions are with other parts of the island of Great Britain.

This was explained away back in 1978. The SNP made two statements at that time: one that the Scottish pound would be of a higher value than sterling, and that the general manager of Standard Life was abusing his position when he pointed out that if that proved to be the case, then his company would have to move its head offices to England. In reply, the chairman of the Associated Life Offices set out the position in a letter to the *Scotsman*, 7 July. Here is the relevant extract:

> Life offices pay their expenses out of loadings in the premiums they collect. About 80 per cent of the loadings received by Scottish Life offices came from England and thus would be paid in English pounds but, because they have their head offices in Scotland, about 70 per cent of their expenses would have to be paid in Scottish pounds. It doesn't require much financial acumen, though obviously a little more than appears to be possessed by certain SNP politicians, to see that if the Scottish pound appreciated against the English pound then the time could arise when a Scottish Life Office would have to move its head office to England.

A Scottish monetary agency – others have done it

That 1978 statement remains valid today, as a pertinent illustration of the importance to the Scottish economy, its businesses and the jobs involved, of the relationship between a Scottish currency and sterling.

That does not mean adopting a policy of absolute one-to-one parity with the Scottish pound hard pegged to sterling, because the price of that would be to require Scotland to have a fiscal position much the same as that of rUK. While such a parity peg would not prevent a Scottish government's budget having different priorities from that of rUK, the broad policy on deficits and borrowing would need to be similar, and so we would have a diminution of the value of independence.

Absolute parity is not necessary, as is proved by the fact that Sottish business, including the financial sector, operates in different countries and different currencies which float on a day-to-day basis. There are ways of offsetting currency fluctuations, and Scottish companies heavily engaged in exporting use them as a normal part of their business planning.

Obviously, it will be necessary for a Scottish authority in charge of currency to manage it in order that no substantial threat is made to business through significant divergence from sterling, but absolute parity is not necessary.

Managing the currency would be the job of a monetary agency (a central bank). Setting that up is not a difficult matter. There are many examples worldwide. What has to be taken into account in doing so, is that its remit has to take into account that Scotland, like Malta (population 440,000), Singapore (5 million) and Hong Kong (7 million), will have a financial system that, due to its international scale, far exceeds the needs of a domestic economy.

Fitch Ratings pointed out that, as the financial crisis unfolded, Malta kept a stable banking system, as did Singapore and Hong Kong, whereas Cyprus, another state with international exposure, did not. There are, therefore, examples of how and how not to create and run a financial system for the Scots to get it right.

Singapore is an excellent guide to what can be done. Its Monetary Authority has successfully managed a flexible currency regime for over thirty years, which has seen it rise from a poor country to one of the world's most successful economies, and that without the vast natural resources available to Scotland.

Scotland has a better balanced economy

Central to currency and monetary policy is the structure of the economy and whether it will support a trade surplus or fail to do so. It is a fact that the Scottish economy is better balanced than, for example, England, as the following table shows:

Breakdown of output by country and broad industry

	England	Scotland	UK
Agriculture	0.6%	1.1%	0.7%
Construction	6.1%	6.4%	6.0%
Production	12.4%	18.1%	14.4%
Services	80.9%	77.4%	78.9%

(SPICE)

Scotland, with specialist engineering, oil, whisky, specialist foods (all integral parts of the economy), exports more than it imports, giving it a substantial balance of trade and current account surplus compared to rUK, which has a chronic balance of payments deficit.

Better Together Claim No. 3: Scotland will have to reapply for membership of the EU

The answer to that claim lies in the question: is it in the interests of an independent Scotland to be a member of the EU? Put another way, why does membership of the EU matter to Scotland?

A yes to the first part of that question just seems to be taken for granted, and certainly the SNP can be considered the most pro-EU party in the UK. As I am primarily responsible for the party's original policy of "Independence in Europe", it may seem strange that I should raise these questions. Given the developments in the EU, treaty by treaty, especially from Maastricht to Lisbon, the question is a pertinent one. Should Scotland have an alternative, even alternatives, to full membership?

Although there were never any outright statements that Scotland would be put out of the EU and find itself at the back of a queue for new membership, Better Together was able to make the most of negative sounds from Spain, the President of the Commission and some others. As we can anticipate facing the same story next time, it is sensible to have more than one position in European negotiations.

It may be, of course, that the result of the coming EU referendum will produce a new situation, but I shall proceed on the assumption that we shall still be talking broadly about the same EU that exists at present.

I raise the question above because the EU of the

1980s, when the SNP policy was formed, is not the EU of today. There were only twelve member states then, the national veto power existed over a very wide range of policies; currency, and matters such as defence, foreign affairs, justice were purely for member states to decide upon. A Scottish seat at the top table would have meaning, and influence. That Europe is no more. It now has twenty-eight member states, and a number of treaties have relegated the national veto to only a few areas. Majority voting has become the norm, economic controls are now in place, and through various treaties a legal and political drive continues to be under way towards a Federal United States of Europe, in which member states would not be sovereign, but subservient to the central organs in Brussels.

The misuse of central power

Great power has transferred to those central organs of the EU, which are essentially undemocratic. Yes, there is an elected Parliament, but *the EU lacks the political and cultural homogeneity* to produce pan-European parties that genuinely span its whole territory, and with which citizens in all states can identify. It is after an election that groups are cobbled together, whereas in the last EU elections, votes were sought by national parties, in our case Labour, Tory, Lib Dem, SNP and UKIP. That is why, when the elite in Brussels talk about the "government" of an "ever closer union" they mean the Commission and the rest of the unelected central apparatus and not a government drawn from the Parliament.

That great central power does not lie dormant. When the Eurozone fell into difficulties, that power was used to unseat democratically elected governments in Greece and Italy, and replace them with unelected technocrats. I am not a blinkered, demented member of UKIP, nor is Ambrose Evans-Pritchard, international business editor of the *Daily Telegraph*, and others who can look at cold facts of misuse of EU power.

In a *Daily Telegraph* article (20 June 2015), his description of the Troika's conduct in Greece, and the ECB's in particular, is worth considering: "The spectacle is astonishing. The European Central Bank, the EMU bail-out fund, and the International Monetary Fund, among others, are lashing out in fury against an elected government that refuses to do what it is told. … Does anybody dispute that the ECB – via the Bank of Greece – is actively inciting a bank run in a country where it is also the banking regulator … . The guardian of financial stability is consciously and deliberately accelerating a financial crisis in an EMU member … as a negotiating tactic to force Greece to the table." He points out that this is not the first time the ECB has sought to organise a "back-room coup d'état" … having parachuted in its vice-president to replace the then Greek prime minister when the latter had the temerity to suggest a referendum on the austerity measure it wanted to impose.

A missing critique

One would have thought that these massive changes, and the conduct of the central organs of the EU, which have had profound effects upon the sovereignty of member states, would have generated critical examination from within the SNP and the wider Scottish community. But not so. We get references about the need for reform, but no substantial analysis of the problems posed by centralised EU power, or policies to combat it.

In her foreword to the government document *Scotland in the European Union*, Nicola Sturgeon noted, "Like many EU governments, the Scottish Government believes the crisis has exposed weaknesses in two areas. Reforms are required both at the level of individual EU policies, to boost economic competitiveness and increase the pace of economic recovery, and at the wider level of the system of EU governance in order to close the 'democratic deficit' that an increasing number of our citizens believes deprives them of an effective say over the nature and content of EU laws and policies." But what reform is needed to meet those objectives? There was no rigorous critique that would, as its conclusion, tell us what "reform" meant.

Popular support for the EU, throughout its territory, has been waning because the treaty changes have weakened the sovereignty of the member states. The claim that member states "share" sovereignty is a fallacy. Sovereignty is transferred, and the transfer of it in the Lisbon Treaty, and in the Eurozone with its Troika visits to Greece and Portugal, where governments were instructed how to act fiscally, cannot be ignored.

Under Lisbon the EU has the sovereign power to sign international treaties and agreements in its own right. How it can exercise that right is a worry. The secrecy with which TTIP negotiations are being conducted is a case in point. Very little is known about what is taking place. Will we only know about this trade agreement when it has been signed?

As Alyn Smith MEP explained to me: "MEPs have access to a locked vault to inspect TTIP documents, but are sworn to secrecy. Even that is a step forward from where we were previously." From what we have been able to gather, sometimes from US sources, unlike WTO, which involves only states, and whose rules were debated in public, TTIP allows large international corporations to shape its terms, and provides them with the power to take governments to a tribunal and overturn policies which have been democratically decided. What are the industrial, commercial, service and public sectors, environmental and health issues being negotiated? We don't know. Although the European Parliament will have a vote to approve or reject it, the final package is likely to be so constructed that the MEPs may find it difficult to reject or amend it. Now that is a question. Will TTIP be presented as a "take it all or none" agreement, or will the EU Parliament be able to amend it?

There are, therefore, legitimate reasons why we should ask that basic question of whether it is in Scotland's interests to be member state?

The answer to a European Union No

Notwithstanding the above critique, it is doubtful if the SNP or others will alter their position to remain in as a member state. But they have to face up to some realities.

First, we have to recognise and openly admit that

Scottish independence, secession of part of a member state, poses genuine problems for the member states and the Commission. At the lowest level of their concerns will be the need for adjustments in the European Parliament as Scotland will be entitled to more seats than at present. An adjustment to the number of commissioners will also be required. Do they enlarge Parliament numbers and commissioners to accommodate more Scots, and who will lose out?

It would seem a small matter to make room for a few extra Scots, but whichever route is chosen may or may not need treaty amendments, and if the latter, that is a road down which none wish to travel, as it would open the door to eurosceptics, not only at Westminster, but in other states as well, to press for substantive changes to how the EU is run. Whether that road is blocked or can be partly opened, we shall see as the UK government negotiates with the EU prior to the in-out referendum. What transpires in those negotiations may have lessons for Scotland next time.

A more substantial problem for the member states is the anxiety about setting a precedent of secession, which is why the Spanish government, facing the Catalonia problem, was vociferous in spelling out that a twenty-eight-member unanimity would be required for Scottish membership. As the EU works on deals between states, and Spain is regarded as one of the big players, it can call in favours from others for this policy.

However, a resolute No to Scotland remaining within the EU as a member state is not without difficulty for the EU as an international institution, whose claim to fame is its democracy. Not only does the EU claim to uphold democracy at home, but it spends a great deal of money promoting it abroad, where it preaches change is always possible so long as it is done through non-violence, a fair election, conducted via a regulated campaign, legal rules, open debate, genuine engagement of the voters, and an honest count.

Would that not be regarded internationally as hypocritical claptrap were it to refuse to recognise and accept a democratic vote in Scotland to change its constitutional relationship with the UK and other EU members? *How could it possibly expel five million of its citizens,* which Scots are by reason of the Lisbon Treaty, for doing what it preaches others to do? Do not do to your own, what you tell others to do. Not exactly the message Brussels would like the world to hear, and laugh at.

Could the EU bob and weave?

Those readers who know only the EU of today will not be aware that in its history, from the creation of the EEC onwards, it has shown a remarkable ability to be politically flexible when confronted with an issue for which there seems to be no solution. The Luxembourg Compromise has long since disappeared from European sight, but it does illustrate that flexibility. When the EEC had only six member states, there was a crisis between France and the others, due to the gradual transition from unanimity to qualified majority voting. France adopted the "empty chair" which meant that when unanimity was required, nothing could be done. That crisis lasted seven months from 30 June 1965.

The Luxembourg Compromise was signed on 30 January 1966 providing, "Where, in the case of decisions which may be taken by majority vote on a proposal of the Commission, very important interests of one or more partners are at stake, the Members of the Council will endeavour, within a reasonable time, to reach solutions which can be adopted by all the Members of the Council while respecting their mutual interests and those of the Community." Or, as one observer said, cutting to the chase, the Compromise gave de facto veto power when any matter was held to be in the national interests of a member state.

What the Compromise demonstrated was that while the Community is based on treaties and legal texts, it also operates at a political level. Another illustration of this political dimension is the Association Agreement with Turkey, signed as long ago as 1963 with an update in 1970. The purpose of the first agreement, as an interim measure, was to facilitate Turkey's accession to the European Community as it was then called. It isn't the various issues involved in trade and technical standards that have prevented Turkey becoming a member of the EU; it is the politics, where a number of member states have indicated that they would oppose Turkey's entry. The barely hidden reason is that Turkey is a Muslim state.

A member who isn't a member?

How could the EU Commission solve the problem it doesn't want to face – perhaps initiating treaty changes and thereby opening up a can of worms – were it to rely on the vote of every one of twenty-eight states to make Scotland a full member?

In *Scotland in the EU*, the SNP government invokes

Article 48 of Lisbon which provides for treaty amend-
ment through "ordinary revised procedure" as the
way in which we shall be admitted. Don't be kidded
by the word "ordinary". Steps available under Article
48 include calling a Convention embracing representa-
tives of national parliaments, the European Parliament,
heads of government, the Commission and even the
European Central Bank. There is a non-Convention
way as well. But no matter which one is taken, they all
end up requiring each member state to ratify what was
agreed. If one says No, no change can happen, and that
way would be blocked for Scotland.

Association Agreement?

Here we come to the question of what is Scotland's
fundamental need in relation to the EU? It is tariff-free
access to the EU market of 500 million people, including the UK. The EU could meet that need short of full
membership through a specially tailored Association
Agreement negotiated while Scotland remained "in",
with no change in trade and other matters during the
negotiations. The text of such an agreement would be
easy to draft, as it would alter nothing in relationships
as Scotland already adheres to all EU requirements for
the single market.

An Association Agreement would also require
twenty-eight member states to accept it. But an agreement of association does not pose the same issues as
does full membership via treaty amendments. By this
method Scotland's trade would continue to have
customs-free access to the EU market, and no doubt

the Common Fisheries Policy would remain intact, as the EU would not want to see that disappear. In fact the existence of the CFP would be a bargaining factor for Scottish negotiators to assist in getting the best Association Agreement possible.

The SNP Scottish government might feel deeply offended, being denied full state membership, when that is the status it desires. But an Association Agreement can be looked at as a gain and not a loss if it sticks to the single market, and goes no deeper into other areas than the Common Fisheries Policy. It is one thing to accept EU directives on single market matters, quite another to accept decisions on international trade with other countries, defence and foreign affairs if Scotland is not a member state.

As well as an Association Agreement, there is another alternative that would secure the same free access to EU markets – membership of the European Free Trade Association (EFTA), and through it membership of the European Economic Area (EEA). The EEA was established in 1994 in a treaty between EFTA members Norway, Iceland and Lichtenstein, and the European Community. Perhaps the EU could request EFTA to admit us to its membership, with the sticky matter of the Common Fisheries Policy accommodated through an EU-Scotland protocol.

EFTA and EEA

EEA membership was referred to in *Scotland in the EU*. This was its conclusion:

The argument that membership of the EEA is desirable because it allows members to gain access to the Single Market but without having to adopt all of the regulations that full EU membership requires is simply wrong. Not only are companies and other economic operators in the EEA countries obliged to adopt all aspects of legislation associated with the single market, they have only very limited input into the decision-making process from which these laws emerge.

The Scottish Government therefore does not consider that EEA membership is a desirable option from a democratic perspective – Scotland's citizens would lose all ability to influence the laws and regulations to which they would be subject.

Note those words "simply wrong" and "lose all ability to influence the laws and regulations to which they would be subject." They are more eloquent rejections of EEA membership than the usual arguments that EFTA countries like Norway and Iceland, because they do not have a vote within the EU, get sent directives and regulations by fax with which they must comply. But the Scottish government's words are just as misleading, more akin to sophisticated propaganda.

The relationship between EFTA states like Norway and the EU in making single market laws is much more complex and inclusive than the "fax" gibe indicates. The agreement between EFTA and the EU in establishing the EEA in 1994 contains 129 articles. Among its provisions is the creation of the EEA Joint Committee and Joint Parliamentary Committee. On the matter of Norway and the other EFTA members' involvement in the making of EU laws, Article 99 states:

1. As soon as new legislation is being drawn up by the EC Commission in a field which is governed by this Agreement, the EC Commission shall informally seek advice from experts of the EFTA States in the same way as it seeks advice from experts of the EC Member States for the elaboration of its proposals.
2. When transmitting its proposal to the council of the European Communities, the EC Commission shall transmit copies thereof to the EFTA States.

    At the request of one of the Contracting Parties, a preliminary exchange of views takes place in the EEA Joint Committee.
3. During the phase preceding the decision of the Council of the European Communities, in a continuous information and consultation process, the Contracting Parties consult each other again in the EEA Joint Committee at the significant moments at the request of one of them.
4. The Contracting Parties shall cooperate in good faith during the information and consultation phase with a view to facilitating, at the end of the process, the decision-taking in the EEA Joint Committee.

Article 100 sets down that "The EC Commission shall ensure experts of the EFTA States as wide a participation as possible according to the areas concerned, in the preparatory stage of draft measures to be submitted subsequently to the committees which assist the EC Commission in the exercise of its executive powers. … When drawing up draft measures the EC Commission shall refer to experts of the EFTA States on the same basis as it refers to experts of the EC Member States."

It is those early stages of drafting EU single market

laws that really matter. By the time legislation gets to the final directive stage, it has been agreed in the processes of consultation, in which EFTA members have taken part. There is no "fax" surprise.

Why "simply wrong" is wrong

Let us consider the claim that it is "simply wrong" to claim that EFTA members are not required to obey all EU single market rules. An EU single market directive required member states and EFTA members to give up their postal services monopoly on letters weighing less than fifty grams, and that such services be put out to tender. Norway rejected the directive.

In 2011 the EU Commission stated that European offshore oil and gas production would be subject to new regulations, and noted that this had "EEA relevance". Norway would not comply. As reported from the EEA Joint Parliament Committee on 27 November 2012, "The Norwegian government has taken the view that the proposed regulation by the European Commission falls outside the geographic and substantive scope of the EEA agreement."

During Iceland's dispute with UK and Holland, the EU backed its two member states by claiming that an EU directive made it compulsory for that small country (with a population of 300,000) to cover the losses of UK and Dutch citizens who had invested in Icelandic banks operating within both countries, when they collapsed in the great financial crash. Gordon Brown used antiterrorist legislation as a means of putting pressure on the Icelandic Government to comply with that directive. Iceland's people, in a referendum, refused to pay up. The EFTA Court, not the EU Court of Justice, found in favour of Iceland.

Another Scottish government error has to be corrected. Page 71 of *Scotland in the EU states*, "EEA countries also make annual financial contributions directly to the EU Budget in return for access to the single market and in order to participate in specific EU policies." We can put that down to loose language or muddled thinking, because "EEA members" embraces EU member states as well as EFTA members. If the government meant EFTA members are committed by compulsion to make payments to the regular EU budget, it was again misleading, and seriously so.

The government is correct in saying EFTA members are required to make a contribution to the EU, but in a very different way to how EU members pay in. EU member states contribute on the basis of an agreed mandatory funding formula. EFTA funding does *not* contribute to the common EU budget. It strengthens EU structural funds through a sum negotiated for a five-year period, and stands separate from the EU budget. In 2009-2014 the sum was €3.27 billion.

EFTA funds come from sovereign states, and are handled through their Financial Mechanism Office which is not part of the EU administration. The EFTA fund deals individually, directly, with the beneficiary EU states – Poland, Romania, Hungary, the Czech Republic, Bulgaria, Lithuania, Slovakia, Latvia, Greece, Portugal, Estonia, Spain, Slovenia, Cyprus, Malta, Croatia.

There are EU budgets to which EFTA can voluntarily contribute. These are specialist areas where cooperation is valuable to all, such as the environment. They are not compulsory. It is at the discretion of EFTA members to contribute or not. As the Norwegian government explains, "When the EEA Joint Committee agrees to incorporate programmes and agencies into the EEA Agreement, Norway commits to making a yearly financial contribution to the relevant EU budget." The operative word is "agrees".

The Scottish government also argued that one advantage of EU membership is that it enables free trade agreements with other countries, as though that were not the case with EFTA membership. EFTA has thirty-five free trade agreements with countries in all parts of the world – Korea, Mexico, Morocco, Turkey, Ukraine, Peru and the Gulf Cooperation Council among them, and one with India under negotiation.

The point that the Scottish government missed is that Norway, Iceland and Lichtenstein are states who exercise sovereignty over a wide range of policies outside the single market not available to a member state of the EU.

Final thoughts on Scotland and the EU

What I have sought to explain is that it would be sensible for the Yes movement, including the Scottish government, to explain to the people that there are alternatives in the event that the EU again adopts a negative attitude to our continued membership. EFTA is one of them.

It is sensible and wise for negotiators to have more than one position in this context. A viable alternative strengthens Scotland's hand with the EU if it says the door to full membership is closed. *But to open up an alternative, and be believed by the EU that it is available, means dialogue with EFTA states should commence now.*

Better Together Claim No. 4: You won't get into NATO without Trident and how will you defend Scotland then?

The answer is a blunt one. Scotland does not need Trident. Scotland does not need NATO, although NATO needs Scotland. UK defence ability is a sham.

The next time we vote on Scottish independence, and are lectured about the threat it would mean to our defence, keep those statements in mind.

In 2014 the SNP government did not ignore defence, devoting eighteen pages to it in the White Paper. But implicit in the way it laid out the likely size and strength of a Scottish Defence Force were the same assumptions that underlie the UK defence establishment's pitch to the people as a means of extracting money from the Treasury for the MOD. That message can be stated simply as "someone out there might like to invade us." Before next time, we not only have to subject that message to a deeper analysis about Scotland's true position in the world, but also peel away any mystique attached to the utterances of the MOD and its generals, admirals and air marshals.

Geopolitical realities
The nuclear powers and their sphere of interests

Nuclear weapons are a deterrent against other states who have them, or in the case of Israel as a deterrent against being overwhelmed by superior conventional forces in a war that would eliminate the state. Should Iran become a nuclear weapons power, Israel would see it as presenting another dimension to its security policy with again its nuclear arsenal as a deterrent to an Iranian attack, just as Iran would see its nuclear arsenal as a deterrent against the USA, using its proxies in the Arab Gulf states and Israel as potential targets.

Which countries holding nuclear weapons pose a threat to Scotland or the UK? North Korea, India, Pakistan, China, France, USA, Russia, Israel? None of these, because there is no threat to them from us, and no reason why they should want to obliterate or conquer us.

Leaving aside the USA and France, friendly powers, all the others with the exception of Russia are wholly Asian powers where, as in nineteenth- and twentieth-century Europe, struggles to maintain balance of power or to gain or prevent hegemony are being played out. The core of world geopolitics has shifted to the Asia-Pacific region.

The USA and Russia have a duality in that setting. Whilst the USA maintains an interest and influence in Europe, it has shifted its main focus to Asia, where it is struggling to develop a long-term policy towards the rising power of China, a China that now aims to have a blue-water fleet, and which is making sovereign claims to areas in the South China Sea – aims that are a cause of concern for America's formal allies, Japan, South Korea and Taiwan, with Vietnam, a historic foe of China, waiting in the US wings. Russia too is an Asian power. The bulk of its population lie in what we would term European territory, but it has a developing involvement in Asia's rise to economic power.

The trigger points of possible conflict are in Asia, with its huge populations, its vast markets, its enormous economic potential, its rise to importance, its unresolved issues between India and Pakistan, and between India and China, and China's claims and counter claims by others. These are what matter to the nuclear powers in that region, not a small Northern European nation of five million people who do not threaten any of them in any way.

Is Scotland threatened with a conventional force invasion?

Which countries with strong enough conventional forces threaten to invade and conquer Scotland and the UK? None. Any invasion of Scotland or the UK by a conventional military force from within Europe but outside the EU would have to be by Russia, as it alone has substantial military power. It would face the most formidable logistical challenges that would make it nigh on impossible. Invasion from any other part of the world would face even more of a nightmare in terms of logistics.

No non-EU European state, Russia or any other, has any reason to contemplate invasion, and other countries such as Turkey, China, Japan, Vietnam, the Philippines, Indonesia and Thailand have their own Middle East and Asian problems to deal with, we are safe. Latin and South American countries are concerned with the USA, not us.

The UK Ministry of Defence and the military establishment know this. But that has not stopped them and their acolytes in the right-wing media drumming up fear of Russia. To maintain military expenditure, the vested interests of the armed forces and their suppliers need us to fear an enemy they can point to and can save us from. Only Russia can fit that bill, so Russia it is.

There have been no direct UK government statements that Russia wants or has any cause to invade Scotland or the UK. Without evidence of intent towards us, the MOD and the generals point to Russia's relations with Ukraine and the Baltic States, and columnists cry "appeasement" if any of us question their views. As the Baltic States are in NATO, any Russian attack would involve a major war. As Putin said on 6 June 2015, "Russia would attack NATO only in [a] mad person's dream."

On the other side, Russian generals are no different from our own lot: they too need a potential enemy to keep being fed more and more cash for more and more armaments. NATO is their choice. So the generals on both sides patrol near each at sea, with aircraft on the Baltic borders, with the Russians even flying down the middle of the English Channel, which apparently they have done for years without complaint, and we are all expected to be on edge, fearful and willing on both sides to feed the military machine.

There isn't a scintilla of evidence that Russia has any purpose or reason to invade the UK or an independent Scotland. In reality, we have no state enemies to be fearful of. Think about it. Have we any reason to invade Russia, or Russia any reason to invade Scotland? When Unionists insist that only by staying under the defence umbrella of the UK are we safe, some are ignorant and others know that claims to the UK's capability of defending this island from invasion are a sham.

UK armed forces hard pushed to defend Cornwall

Lord Dannatt, former Army Chief of Staff recently lamented the state of the British armed forces, pointing out that with an army reduced to eighty-thousand, able to put only one division into a battlefield, a Royal Navy reduced to nineteen warships, and an air force down to a number of squadrons you could count on two hands, they have never been weaker.

The imperial mind still exists, and in the campaign led by the *Daily Telegraph* and Tory MPs to boost defence expenditure to 2% of GDP, columnist after columnist has declaimed that figure as necessary so that the UK remains a "world power". The status they hanker after requires a state to be able to do two things – have sufficient conventional forces at home to defend it without resorting to self-annihilation via a nuclear exchange, and project independent military power abroad. The UK can do neither.

An army capable of putting only one division in the

field, around twenty thousand, with few RAF squadrons to help, would be hard pushed to defend Cornwall, and the Royal Navy hard pushed to defend the Isle of Wight. Everyone in the UK MOD and the Pentagon knows, and some have admitted publically, that UK forces cannot operate effectively abroad unless it is in partnership with the United States.

Dumb turkeys

Next time, Yes Scotland should take the so-called military experts head on. Looked at in the cold light of facts, they should be a laughing stock. They have committed to two aircraft carriers, but can only be certain of commissioning one into service. But the one coming into service, the Queen Elizabeth, has no aircraft. These, the F-35s, are not expected to be available until 2020, but that is problematical. They can fly, but modern fighter aircraft need to do more than that.

During live flight-testing the Pentagon discovered deficiencies in the plane's software, affecting its warfare ability, weapon delivery accuracy, use of radar, friend-or-foe identification, electro-optical targeting and navigation. There were other problems too.

In a scathing article in *The Herald* in March 2015, Robie Dinwoodie laid bare the fiasco of the F-35 to be bought from the Americans. Despite $400 billion spent so far in its development the plane is not operational, and as Dinwoodie reported it has been described by one aviation expert as "inherently terrible, based on a dumb idea, astonishingly unmanoeuvrable and not good at anything, a turkey". A dumb turkey. The MOD?

The scandal of defeat covered up – at a cost of lives

It is not only on procurement that we should feel able to assail the MOD and its generals and admirals, who will come to lecture us again. Their army was defeated in Iraq and Afghanistan, not because the junior officers, NCOs and other ranks were of lesser calibre than those who fought in WWII, Korea or the Falklands, but because the level of political direction and senior officer command was abysmal.

Young men and women were put into danger because of incompetence. They were given a task in post-war Iraq that they were not equipped for. In Afghanistan the Defence Secretary, now Lord John Reid, boasted that no British soldier would "fire a single shot". The troops fired forty-six million rounds. As Maj. Gen. Andrew Mackay (one of the better ones) put it, they went into to Helmand with "eyes shut and fingers crossed". Lt Col. Richard Williams, a former commander of the SAS, wrote in the *Times* on 28 October 2014, "A Chilcot-style inquiry is needed into the glaring inadequacies of the British military command over 13 years" in Afghanistan. We have still to see whether the Chilcot inquiry has been worth the six years' wait for its findings on Blair's invasion of Iraq.

This is what Lt Col. Williams had to say, "Commanding the Helmand operation in the same broken way that we commanded the Iraq operation – from a bunker outside London rather than in Kabul alongside our allies, risked confusion and was arrogant madness. ... To allow a very aggressive and impeccably impressive commander of Task Force Helmand in 2006 to extend the scope of his military operations beyond the limit of the nation's ability to support them appears to be an abject failure of generalship at the level above him." The impeccably dressed officer was Brigadier Ed Butler.

The House of Commons Defence Committee has stated that British soldiers were left "dangerously exposed" in Helmand because forces chiefs "grossly underestimated" the scale of Taliban resistance, and that "those responsible did not seem to have sought the right expert advice, or if they did, ignored it." Those responsible were not only the senior military officers, but their civilian political masters. The report noted that one cabinet minister "was not aware of being in the chain of command."

Next time we in the Yes movement are lectured, just spell out the non-achievements of the Ministry of Defence and its expert military advisers: an army that cannot operate on its own abroad without being part of a USA adventure, and is unable to mount a serious defence of the homeland, and a navy that cannot let its flagship carriers out of dock, because it may not have aircraft on board.

The real reason the UK hangs on to Trident

Out of four nuclear missile submarines, one is always at sea. The missiles are not aimed at anyone. Trident is a weapon of mass destruction, and as such immoral, but it is not intended for use militarily, as the direct threats posed to the UK are from non-state actors like al-Qaeda, ISIL and other Islamic terrorists, who take no notice of the nuclear might sailing below sea level. Were it by some mischance to blow them all up (along with the rest of us), they would be happy, believing that within a second they would land in Paradise.

Trident is a political weapon now, in the arena of the UN Security Council. Having a nuclear weapon, as do the other four permanent veto-wielding members, is seen as important in Westminster. There is no other reason that would justify a declining state with sixty million of a population keeping its seat, when countries like India, Brazil, Germany, Japan and Indonesia are excluded. Tory MP Alan Duncan once blurted out on radio that without Trident, "We would lose our Security Council seat."

As seen from Westminster, Trident keeps them at the topmost top table in the world. Being a permanent member means the British Foreign Office matters; it is one of the reference points for other countries to talk to, lobby, especially as the UK is seen as very close to that other permanent member, the USA. Take away that seat, and who would beat a path to the UK Foreign Secretary? No one. Avoiding a monumental crash in status, this is what is at stake with Trident. The cost of the UK's continued presence on the Security Council, is that Scotland keeps Trident.

Westminster governments may be happy to pay that entry price, but not at our expense.

Who needs NATO?

As we have no state enemies, Scotland should look at defence in a different light from what has been regarded as the norm in Cold War days. NATO and the Warsaw Pact were set up because both sides suspected the other of potential aggression. Post Cold War, with the archives opening up, it seems that the USSR's policy was to hold the Eastern European countries as a buffer against any move to invade by the West, rather than as a launching pad for aggression, while the West saw NATO as a defensive shield in case the Soviets invaded Western Europe. A great deal of money and scientific effort were expended on both sides to prevent what one thought the other intended, but was never intended by either.

Russia, in its days of empire, or now shorn of it, has always feared invasion from the West. It has good grounds for this. The Soviet archives show that Stalin's policy, just like the czars before him, was to create a buffer zone in Eastern Europe as part of Soviet security. That is a legitimate geopolitical policy, just as legitimate as the age-old British foreign policy of maintaining a balance of power in Europe for its security. Even in this age of continental missiles, geography still counts.

There are those who would contest that any state has legitimate geopolitical needs that necessitate extending its influence or physical presence into another territory. That view flies in the face of all human history. State interests, spheres of influence and geopolitical realities determined state conduct in the centuries BC, and have done and will continue to do so in the centuries AD.

Russia is not the enigma wrapped in Churchill's mystery

There is in the West a large body of expertise and knowledge about the true state of Russian mentality in geopolitical terms, yet our people are still fed on a diet of ideas that depict Russia as just waiting to invade.

One of those experts, Robert D Kaplan, tells us in his book *The Revenge of Geography*, "Insecurity is the quintessential Russian national emotion" arising from its history and the influence of geography on that history (p. 159). Kaplan is a US establishment figure, having served on the US Defense Policy Board and, among other things in a distinguished career studying geopolitics, has been visiting professor at the US Naval Academy, Annapolis. He is not a soft pinko. He writes, "For what drove the Soviet Union to carve out an empire in Eastern Europe at the end of World War II still holds today: a legacy of depredations against Russia by Lithuanians, Poles, Swedes, Frenchmen, and Germans, leading to the need for a cordon sanitaire of compliant regimes in the space between historic Russia and Central Europe" (p. 150).

Kaplan is not alone in his assessment of Russia. Thomas Graham, a former staff member of the US National Security Council, whose job was to study Russia, had this to say in a *Financial Times* article published on 31 May this year:

> The West acts as if it had a Vladimir Putin problem. In fact it has a Russia problem. The Russian President stands within a long tradition of Russian

thinking. His departure would fix nothing. Any plausible successor would pursue a similar course, if perhaps with a little less machismo. ... European states seek security in balance; Russia seeks it in strategic depth. That view grows out of its location on the vast, nearly featureless great Eurasian plain, across which armies have moved with ease.

The point Kaplan and Graham were making is that history and geography leave their mark on peoples. Take the UK as an example. The remembrance events in respect of the First World War, one hundred years ago, show that with its huge losses it remains lodged in the British public mind. World War II is still important in our collective life. Consider the effect of that war on the peoples and policymakers in Russia today. This is the catalogue of destruction suffered by the USSR:

Thirty per cent of national wealth destroyed. 8.7 million combat dead, 19 million civilian dead.

Totally destroyed: 1,710 towns, 70,000 villages, 32,000 factories, 285,000 livestock buildings, 35,000 threshing machines, 5 million kW of power, 45,000 textile machines, 84,000 schools, 98,000 collective farms looted, 4,100 railway stations, 6,000 hospitals, 33,000 clinics, 1,500 specialised high schools, 334 institutes of higher education, 43,000 libraries, 427 museums, 167 theatres, 65,000 kms of rail lines, 13,000 km of rail bridges, 15,000 locomotives, 428,000 railcars, 1,400 ships, 8,300 river vessels, 2,078 km of telegraph and telephone lines, 7 million horses killed, 17 million cattle killed.

Nothing brings home the full extent of the sacrifice more

than the fact that of the young men born in the USSR in 1923, 80% perished in the fight against the Nazis.

Far from wanting to launch a new war against the West in 1945, the priority for the USSR was restoring that damage, and the last thing the Soviets needed was to become embroiled in another war in Europe. Memoirs and archives have shown that Stalin and his successors were deeply suspicious of Western intentions, and that they were committed to an ideological struggle, not a military one, with the US and its allies. Both the USSR and the USA were prepared to conduct proxy wars, but not a war over either Western European or Soviet territory. This of course is hindsight. The fear that created the Cold War and NATO-Warsaw pacts was real for decision-makers at that time, on both sides.

Has NATO got any real role any longer?

NATO is a Cold War construct, and although the Cold War is over, it remains part of the military-industrial complex that President Eisenhower warned about as he left office in 1960. There are too many political, military and arms industry vested interests for the idea of redundancy to be in its collective mind. To keep it in being, it has sought an out-of-area role in the Balkans and Afghanistan; not very successfully in the latter. Earlier this year, however, the war drum was being beaten in NATO HQ. It had found a reason for existing, a potential enemy, an old enemy, in Russia.

Russia has breached international law with its

annexation of Crimea, and its involvement in that part of Ukraine on its borders, rather in the same way NATO interfered in Serbia and carved out Kosovo in breach of that law. Two blacks and no white among them. Putin's Russia is not only unpleasant for gays and those of a liberal outlook, but a dangerous place for those who oppose the Kremlin. However, it is important to separate the regime from what are, even if Putin was replaced by a saint, Russia's national interests.

The broken pledge

When Gorbachev decided that holding Eastern Europe hostage to the foreign policy of the USSR was unsustainable and over, he met the US Secretary of State Baker to agree what would follow, knowing those countries would travel swiftly into the Western sphere. Gorbachev's chief concern was the continued existence of the buffer zone.

He got Baker's agreement that none of the Eastern European countries would be allowed to join NATO, because if they did, there would be no buffer zone, and the Soviet Union, especially the Russian part, would find a foreign military alliance right on its borders. The then US Ambassador to the Kremlin, Jack Matlock Jr., took notes at the meeting. Baker gave the assurance Gorbachev asked for, and Matlock's notes record Baker saying that NATO would not advance "an inch" to the east. It advanced much more than that inch.

That broken pledge is the root of Russia's antagonism to the West today. Those Eastern European countries are in NATO, and the alliance is on the borders of Russia. The invitation to Georgia to join NATO by President George W. Bush caused the Russians to invade that country to stop it happening. Russia found the EU invitation to Ukraine to join in a special relationship alarming, because it sees that as paving the way to membership of NATO.

In December 2014 the Ukrainian parliament repealed the law banning participation in military alliances. President Poroshenko commented: "Ukraine's non-aligned status is out." A NATO spokesman took note and said: "Our door is open and Ukraine will become a member of NATO if it so requests and fulfils the standards and adheres to the necessary principles."

Russia, if Ukraine lined up with NATO, would find its Black Sea fleet based in Crimea in a rather awkward situation, to put it mildly. Russia could not allow that to happen any more than, in the 1960s, the USA could permit Soviet missiles to lodge in Cuba.

No one has ever answered the question why NATO went back on its word to Gorbachev, who kept his. Nor has anyone ever explained why NATO, with the Cold War over, needs to stand on the borders of Russia.

Some apologists for NATO expansion eastwards have argued that the Baltic States, Poland and the others are perfectly entitled to apply for membership. Of course they are. Their recent experience as vassals of the Soviet Union means they will look for an alliance that can protect them. But their legitimate geopolitical concerns have to be balanced with Russia's, the Western nations' relationship with Russia, and, above all, that NATO pledge. That the Eastern European states were enabled to join NATO is what lies at the heart of the present impasse with Russia, a Russia that believes it was deceived by the United States on behalf of NATO.

Russia's reaction, especially to Ukraine's move westwards, is a gift to the generals and others in NATO. Where will Russia stop? Crimea today, the Baltic States tomorrow they ask? Or Romania where NATO military exercises were held in May of this year? As Chapter 5 of the NATO Charter declares, an attack on one is an attack on all; we have to have a military posture in those "threatened" states, although NATO has had to admit that there has not been one incursion in the Baltic States' airspace, or in any other NATO member, by a Russian plane.

Dismal diplomacy

The way the Russian celebration on the seventieth anniversary of VE day in 2015 was reported in the British media is instructive. The parade of Russian military power in Red Square was reported, with suitable comment about Russian involvement in Ukraine, but not a single picture was broadcast of the 500,000-civilian parade, of people holding up photographs of those who fought and died in World War II. In that parade were not only Russians but other nationalities, among them British and other Western war veterans. An extraordinary, poignant, moving human event, which did not merit reporting by the UK media. It did not fit the narrative of a Russia just waiting to pounce on the West.

What we have in NATO is an organisation whose diplomacy has been abysmal, the result of which has created problems that would not have existed between

Europe and Russia had there been a proper under-standing of Russian anxieties, and no advancement of NATO eastwards.

The SNP, not just its government, took a decision to reverse its opposition to NATO membership, despite deeply held views on nuclear weapons. The party majority believed, and I agreed with them, that removing a question mark over our involvement with it would ensure that NATO would not take a position opposing independence. We were wrong. I hope the lesson has been learned.

The SNP does not need to make that mistake again. Nor does anyone else in Scotland. Scotland has no state enemies to be afraid of, to be defended from. Scotland has been NATO's northern land based aircraft car-rier from which air power can cover the Icelandic gap against any incursion from the North Sea into the sea lanes of the Atlantic by a hostile fleet (that could only be the Russian Northern Fleet). The Warrior exercise held around Scotland in April was based on our strate-gic position within NATO, but NATO says we cannot join it. The question now is who would want to?

It is doubtful, notwithstanding the speeches from the officer class and those companies who need the mili-tary contracts, whether NATO is the defence organi-sation it is cracked up to be. In Norway last year, in an exercise of the NATO rapid reaction force, meant to be a message to Russia over Ukraine, German soldiers used broomsticks painted black instead of guns, and it has been reported that the German military was using Mercedes vans as stand-ins for armoured personnel car-riers during training, because of equipment shortages.

If that is the NATO that doesn't want us, so be it. It is no loss to us.

Real defence needs

What real threats does Scotland face? Not invasion by an external military power. We do not have a perfect harmonious society, but there is an excellent relationship and bonding between those with a long Scottish ancestry, Irish-Scottish ancestry, Italian, Chinese, Polish, Spanish, Islamic Scots and others. Yet, due to our history as part of imperial Britain, and due to recent interventions in other countries, we have not been free from terrorism in our domestic life, and given the nature of extreme political Islam, as evidenced by the hatred shown by ISIL and others for everything in the West, we cannot be sure we are safe from them and their adherents.

In the economic field, our fisheries resources, and the integrity and safety of the oil and gas rigs in the North Sea are both areas where physical defence is required in the shape of military hardware and personnel. Our long coastline has proved on occasion to be attractive to large-scale drug smugglers, and that too needs a combination of intelligence and equipment.

As NATO does not want Scotland, and Scotland does not need NATO, our international position should be that of neutrality. Across the water is another neutral small state, Ireland, and we can take it as a benchmark. Neutrality does not mean military impotence. Ireland has contributed its forces to United Nations peacekeeping duties in various parts of the world, such as Congo, Chad, East Timor and Lebanon. These are not easy duties, and require highly trained professional personnel.

Taking Ireland as a benchmark, and taking account of geography and the size and importance of the oil and gas industry offshore, Scotland will need a small highly efficient full-time defence force of about ten thousand strong. Fisheries and coastal defence would require twelve specialised naval vessels (which should keep the Clyde shipbuilders busy), plus twelve helicopters, two maritime patrol aircraft and eight turboprop aircraft.

At the core of that defence force must be a Special Operations Group, of the standard of the SAS, capable of dealing with any terrorist threat on Scottish soil or offshore.

As our forces would not be engaged with NATO responsibilities and costs, our defence budget will be much lower than the £4 billion we contribute towards UK defence spending at present. As an independent Scotland will own a large military real estate and bases, there will be no need for costly construction of military infrastructure. It should be possible to shed some real estate into the market for housebuilding at a profit.

It is not so much physical attacks nations like ours face, but cyber attacks on national computer systems that serve power stations, communications, hospitals, other essential services and the banking system.

Those are the real threats to which we must fashion a defence. It means that Scotland's governments must have a different defence policy to that of the UK. Nostalgia for being a world power drives UK policy, whereas our future lies in being a small, democratic, neutral country devoted to assisting others in the international community.

Better Together Claim No. 5: Independence would put Scotland's security at risk

During the referendum we had the pleasure of listening to the Home Secretary warn that independence would place us in jeopardy because we would cease to shelter under the UK system operated by MI5, MI6 and GCHQ's universal surveillance capabilities. Implicit in that lecture was that after independence, Scotland would be treated differently from many other foreign countries with which the UK security services cooperate in the struggle against terrorism. Are we to take such drivel seriously?

In answering that, we have to explain that Scotland does not get that security apparatus for nothing today. We pay our share of it, and that money will be spent after independence up here, to fund our own system. We shall build upon those security system structures already in Scotland which we shall inherit. As for being isolated in security terms, it would be absurd for any Westminster government, which got information from GCHQ of a threat, refusing to share it with Scottish authorities given the shared border, just as it would be perverse for Scottish security organs to refuse to cooperate with those south of the border with information gained up here. Security threats cross borders, and national security services respond with international cooperation.

Better Together Claim No. 6: Transition costs will be huge

Building upon the present security system which exists within Scotland will be one of the transition costs which the No side made so much of in the referendum. A ping-pong argument developed between Better Together and the SNP government with figures ranging from £600 million to £2 billion batted back and forth.

The answer which the No side would not grasp, and Yes put over somewhat inadequately, if the questions I got at meetings were any guide, is that a transition cost is just that: a one-off from one position to another. It is not repeated. Given the savings Scotland will make on defence expenditure, the transition costs, even if around £2 billion, will be worth it.

Better Together Claim No. 7: Scotland will be lumbered with its share of UK national debt

Money spent on us, as in the other parts of the UK, has been borrowed. It seems obvious that Scotland should take a share of that accumulated national debt on independence. But that *position has to be qualified by a number of factors, the chief of which is that we need to enter negotiations with Scottish state interests at the heart of them. Those state interests are to emerge from negotiations with the smallest possible share of the debt.*

State interests are not something Scots have bothered

much about in the last three hundred years, leaving such to the governments in Westminster. Independence is about creating a Scottish state, a sovereign power, with interests of its own to advance and defend. So, if we are to be serious about creating a Scottish state, we have to place our state interests into any equation of relations with other states, and that must be the guiding principle of our negotiations with England over a division of assets and liabilities.

The debt and the discount on it

UK national debt at time of writing stands at over £1.5 trillion. So, how do we face a demand that we take a share of it, and how do we avoid lumbering ourselves with more debt inheritance than necessary?

We start with a fact: because the UK government has told the financial markets that it, and it alone, will stand good for the debt, we are not bound legally to burden ourselves with a penny of it. We still have to deal with the moral aspect, but that is the legal position.

During the referendum when this was pointed out, the No side declared that Scotland independent would start off with the reputation for defaulting. A foolish assertion. You can only default on debt acknowledged by creditors as yours, and owing to them. As the UK Treasury has placed the burden on itself, irrespective of a referendum result, there would be no such creditor acknowledgement unless our negotiators on behalf of Scotland committed to taking on a share.

But taking state interests into account and that we are not legally bound is a strong bargaining hand when we come not only to the moral principle of taking a share, but crucially deciding what that share will be. It is vital for Scotland in creating a new state, to create new economic structures in place of the failed ones we have experienced as part of the UK, that we drive down our share of the debt. We can do so legitimately.

Should we take our 8.3% of the £1.5 trillion? An emphatic no, for a number of reasons. First there is a lot of funny money in that debt. A consequence of quantitative easing (printing money electronically) is that the Bank of England holds £325 billion worth of its own UK Government debt. The government pays interest on that debt to the bank, but in 2012-13 the chancellor engaged in a new wheeze: he transferred the accumulated interest from the bank back to the Government's account. The sum involved was £35 billion.

If after Scotland signed up to take our share of the £1.5 trillion, the UK government cancelled that £325 billion held by the Bank of England (32% of total national debt), or it just stayed dormant forever (as good as cancelled), we would be left as suckers, holding more debt per head than the Westminster Government.

Removing that Bank of England holding from the debt share-out assessment will reduce Scotland's inherited debt. There are other factors. Trident will be on notice to quit, but that cannot be done immediately the notice is issued. Perhaps it will take four or five years for the UK government to find and build another location. Trident cannot sit rent-free, and if the UK government seeks a period of four or five years before shifting it, then we should require a debt discount in lieu of rent.

There is another aspect to Trident that should be

brought into play in Scottish debt reduction. Oil was found in the Firth of Clyde in early 1981, at a time when Margaret Thatcher's Tory government was destroying Scotland's industrial base. Scots were kept in ignorance of it, but oil companies knew about it. BP sought and got a production licence (No. PL262) to explore and develop the oil.

Exploration and development of an oilfield in the Clyde would have been a new industry offering jobs right long the Renfrewshire-Ayrshire coast and right down to Galloway. It didn't happen because of Trident. On 17 September 1981 the Ministry of Defence informed the Department of Energy and the Scottish Office of its "blanket refusal to agree to any rig under any circumstances" in order that nuclear submarines could navigate safely through our waters. The West of Scotland, unknown to its people, paid a heavy price for Trident. There should be another reduction in our share of the debt for the enormous benefits that were denied to our communities, while we paid the social and health costs of high unemployment in that part of Scotland.

Then there is the oil wealth we never got, the oil wealth that was known but denied, the oil wealth that we were lied to about, the oil fund we should have had, but did not get. That too is worth a discount.

If any Unionist says that Westminster will never agree to those demands, the answer is simple: it is to repeat that Scotland has no legal obligation to accept a share of UK debt given that the UK government has assured the markets that it and it alone is responsible for every pound of that £1.5 trillion. It is Scotland that has the strong negotiating hand, and it is in our national interests to play it to the full.

Better Together Claim No. 8: ... or how did we lose the pensioners?

The answer here is to tell truth against lies, and do so with vigour. In a cleverly worded letter from Gordon Brown to pensioners during the referendum, he wrote of his anxiety about the "UK pension fund" and the threat to continuity of state pension payments. That letter clearly implied that a Yes vote would put the state pension in jeopardy.

It was clever, because there is no UK pension fund in the sense that "fund" has a meaning in the pensions world, that is money invested to build up huge capital sums from which pensions are paid. Our National Insurance contributions do go into a National Insurance Fund, but are not used to build up a "fund" in that sense, as happens in company pension schemes.

National Insurance contributions have a dual purpose. One is to provide qualification for a state pension, and the other is to use the money that comes in, to pay out to pensions. There are no investments. It is an in-out system. When working I paid my father's pension, now my children in work pay my pension, and when they retire their children will pay their pensions out of their NI contributions. Brown knew that, and yet his deliberate reference to a "fund", while linguistically correct, carried a sinister meaning, and did nothing to convey the reality that underlines state pension payments in an in-out system.

Brown, a former chancellor and prime minister, and still an MP at that time, knew that state pensioners had nothing to fear from independence, because the

UK government had issued this statement, in January 2013, making clear that there was no threat:

> If Scotland does become independent this will have no effect on your State Pension, you will continue to receive it just as you do at present.

Here I think the Yes campaign erred. I cannot recall pensioners receiving an individual letter from the Yes side, carrying that vital quote from the DWP, along with an explanation that where a person lives is irrelevant to the contractual, legal right to a state pension. Many people have gone to France, Spain, Portugal and many other countries, to live there permanently on retirement. They get the UK state pension as of right.

What is true about the state pension is true about company pensions. They are not paid on the basis of country of residence, but on a contractual legal right.

The Yes campaign met pensioner resistance (75% voted No) based on the fear generated by Brown and others, but not enough was done to drive home the truth; not enough done to publicise that DWP letter, to make sure it was read and understood by every pensioner in Scotland. Appeals by Yes activists to grannies, grandpas, aunts and uncles to think and vote for the younger generation were outweighed in many a pensioner mind by the fear of losing the pension.

That is understandable. Pensioners are wide open to manipulation by the fearmongers, because as the years advance, they lose earning power. Reliance on the state pension, little as it is, becomes their lifeline. Lose it, and absolute poverty beckons. Until that fear is removed, many pensioners will act solely in their own interests. There is no point in getting angry at those who take this position, as opposed to voting for the grandchildren's future. People are going to live much longer in future years, and so their financial vulnerability is something they cannot ignore. That is the reality the next campaign has to address.

There is one organisational idea to be taken on board now – at national level Yes must have a pensioner unit supplying local campaigns with facts, and ensuring that national advertising in newspapers has to get the "your pension is safe" message across. Every local Yes campaign must also have a pensioner unit, whose sole purpose is to identify where pensioners live, talk to as many of them as possible to trace the effects of fear, and produce the truth in letters and leaflets that prove their pensions are safe.

Better Together Claim No. 9: Scotland cannot count on the oil ... there's not that much left

The most remarkable achievement of the Unionist Better Together campaign was to turn the great national asset of North Sea oil into a negative for the Yes campaign. Their charge that it's volatile on price, it is not what it used to be, there is less of it than claimed, and you cannot put all our economic eggs in the oil basket worked a treat for them. The answer is in spreading *knowledge* widely of oil and energy policy. Next time we shall have to be much more robust in answering, and doing so will require knowledge we do not at present have.

That experience of oil in the referendum was not the

first time that the Scots allowed themselves to be gulled about the value of oil. As soon as it was discovered in the 1970s, two versions of its importance emerged: one for the mugs in the north, and another for the people in the south. In Scotland the oil find was decried as not as important as the SNP claimed. We were told it would not last long, that you could not rely upon it and, the old one that appeared again during the referendum, that it wasn't really Scotland's oil, but Shetland's, and what would happen if Shetland departed from Scotland. You will not have heard of Shetland departing since the referendum, but it is always there to be fished out again in future.

The story of how Scots were robbed is one that historians of our country will wonder about in years to come, when all the government files are opened, and they can read back on how our media fell in with the Westminster plot. While Scots were being told to forget the oil, a secret report was written, in February 1974, by Dr. Gavin McCrone, Chief Economic Adviser to the Scottish Office. In that report he examined the claims made by the SNP and came to the conclusion that they were too modest. As his report said, "An independent Scotland could now expect to have massive surpluses both on its budget and on its balance of payments … this situation could last for a very long time into the future. … For the first time since the Act of Union was passed, it can now be credibly argued that Scotland's economic advantage lies in its repeal." No wonder that was kept secret. Not a single whistleblower anywhere, including Scottish labour ministers.

Ignorance is not bliss

The fact that the public had been well and truly mesmerised, lied to, and softened up in all the years before 2014 made it relatively easy for Better Together to promote the wrong story about oil. As a nation with vast amounts of oil discovered in its waters, we are remarkably ignorant of an industry that sends some forty million tonnes of the stuff into the world each year, and employs around 450,000 people in the UK. There are a number of expert Scots who know the industry, but most of us are in total ignorance. How many fields are under production? Where does the oil go in the world market? Why is Brent Crude an industry price benchmark? Who are the companies operating there? How many rounds of licensing have been issued? Who has licences for exploration not yet operable? What do those licences say? How many platforms are working, and where were they built? I asked a taxi driver and he said twenty; there are hundreds. How many are due for decommissioning and where will that take place? Outside of the experts, the rest of us do not know the answers.

Ignorance is not bliss. Knowledge is power, and we have been kept well away from knowledge about the North Sea, and so are wide open to a propaganda barrage that tells us oil is a problem rather than an asset. The Scottish economy does not and will not rest solely on the oil industry. In terms of how we can use it to advantage, the contribution it makes to GDP, and its ability to generate jobs and advance Scotland in the scientific areas, it is of great importance.

So effective has been the propaganda that the Scots become highly sensitive and uncomfortable when claims are made about the importance of oil to Scotland. This came home to me time after time during the referendum campaign, when I deliberately spent time on the issue in my speeches. I could feel the audience was uncomfortable, not wanting, as Better Together told them, to put too much emphasis on its value.

The Sir Ian Wood intervention

Yes activists in the social media tried hard to combat the oil negativity, but what was lacking was an authoritative rebuttal of the Unionist tale of woe. That did not happen. It was the case that a good part of the formal Yes campaign kept its head down on oil, and sadly when Sir Ian Wood came out with the claim that only fifteen billion barrels remained to be harvested, instead of rubbishing him and his forecast, praise was heaped upon him as an expert even by some on the Yes side. In his own report to the UK government, Wood placed the reserves as between twelve and twenty-four billion barrels, but no one asked why he chose the bottom range when his own report showed that, if his recommendations were followed, it was twenty-four billion.

A key recommendation of his report was a strong regulator, one of whose functions would be to get the industry to commit to "greater collaboration in key areas such as the development of regional hubs, sharing of infrastructure, appropriate sharing of geophysical information and the reduction of the complexity and delays in current legal and commercial processes." A potential additional benefit of £200 billion was identified from this kind of collaboration. That regulator, Oil and Gas Authority, was put in place on 1 April 2015, as an executive agency of the Department of Energy & Climate Change. It will become a wholly-owned government company in 2016.

Now the referendum is safely out of the way, the real amount of oil still to be had from the North Sea can emerge. It is twenty-three billion barrels. The source for the twenty-three billion? None other than UK Oil & Gas, the industry's collective organisation. That figure, of course, takes no account of the giant Clair Ridge field found west of Shetland. It is interesting to note that in the statement announcing its second annual conference in 2015, UK Oil & Gas did not mention the Clair Ridge.

Clair Ridge

A press release by BP on 25 June 2015, headlined "First Clair Ridge Topside Modules Safely Installed West of Shetland" *told us that because of new extraction technology "the Clair Ridge development will have the capability to produce an estimated 640 million barrels of oil over a 40 year period, with peak production expected to be up to 120,000 barrels of oil per day."*

Clair Ridge did not seem to enter Sir Ian Wood's assessment of Scotland's oil potential, nor did we hear it trumpeted during the referendum by BP and its partners ConocoPhillips, Chevron and Shell. One thing we should remember from the intervention of BP and others in the oil industry is that they will hide the truth, and lie along with other Unionists when confronted with the possibility of Scottish control through independence.

Big oil & small nation – time to understand the implications

What remains in the North Sea, assuming no other finds, will last for forty years, and the Clair Ridge find will itself last for that length of time. That is something Scots should ponder, especially in relation to the point I am just about to make, a point that for some strange reason has never been widely grasped by our nation.

What was never explained to the Scots, and must be explained long before we enter into another referendum, is that the oil in the North Sea and west of Shetland is far more valuable an asset to five million people of an independent Scotland than it is to sixty million in the UK. A good analogy is the Euro lottery. If a syndicate of sixty people win the £10 million prize it is worth £166,666.66 each. But if five people have the winning ticket, it is worth £2 million each.

The UK is now a major net importer of oil and gas. An independent Scotland will remain a net exporter, the only one in the EU. It is estimated that 60% of oil deposits in the EU are in Scotland. The UK is not self-sufficient in energy. An independent Scotland will be, not only with oil but other forms of energy production. That means a different oil extraction policy, structured to Scotland's long-term interests.

That volatile stuff

Much was made by the Unionists of the collapse in oil prices when Brent Crude went down to just over $47 a barrel. Didn't that prove their point? Were not all calculations by the SNP now rendered foolish? Well no. Although oil and water do not mix, oil and politics do. The reason for the price collapse was due to Saudi Arabia, the swing producer, keeping its taps wide open for two reasons: one was to drive down the market share of the shale oil producers in the USA, and the other was to put the squeeze on Iran during the negotiations about its nuclear future. It has the additional benefit, for its western allies, of putting the squeeze on Russia over Ukraine.

But, as industry commentators were arguing as far back as January 2015, the downward pressure on price could not continue. The price of Brent Crude rose to $65.39 in May 2015, and at the time of writing it stands at $61.55.

That price of $61.55 at July 2015 has to be compared to the following table which shows that while oil did rise to over $100, the price was out of kilter with other years, when the volatility was less dramatic:

Brent Crude Spot Price FOB US dollars per barrel

July 2005	57.52	July 2011	116.97
July 2006	73.67	July 2012	102.62
July 2007	76.93	July 2013	107.93
July 2008	132.72	July 2014	106.77
July 2009	64.44	July 2015	61.55
July 2010	75.78		

When you strip out the years 2011-2014, which were due to geopolitical events such as the chaos in Libya and disruption elsewhere, although the 2015 price is lower than what might be termed "normal" years, it remains a profitable level at around the price the industry is planning for (see below for UK Oil & Gas's viewpoint). The North Sea, in terms of exploration and production, is an expensive place to operate, and the industry is making efforts to reduce costs. The Wood Report, already referred to, made a number of sensible recommendations for improving performance in the North Sea. UK Oil & Gas reported that as part of the response to the reduction in price, the industry is employing measures to drive down the cost of production per barrel.

Even as the Unionists were celebrating the lower price of oil, there were voices warning that such would not be the case in immediate future years. They pointed out that cutbacks in investment at a time when, despite the problems faced by various countries, world economic growth would continue, mean that the demand for oil would increase, and upward pressures on price be restored. As was noted by Andrew Critchlow in the *Daily Telegraph* (17 January 2015), "In the current rush to predict a floor to the oil prices it is easy to forget that over the next 25 years rising populations and economic growth will require significantly more energy." He points out that "Opec itself expects oil prices to be somewhere in the region of $177 per barrel by 2040 as the world will require 111m bpd of crude, up from just over 91m bpd at present."

Critchlow was far from being alone. A range of people, including Claudio Descalzi, CEO of Italy's oil company Eni, and Fatih Birol, chief economist of the

International Energy Agency, have warned that investment pauses in developing new fields could result in future oil prices soaring up to and above the $100 level. Descalzi has an interest in that happening.

Forecasting oil prices is not a science. I recall a famous UK White Paper in the 1960s which claimed that oil would remain stable at $3 a barrel!

In a speech on 17 June 2015, Deirdre Michie, chief executive of UK Oil & Gas, pointed out: "Over the last 20 years, the price has averaged at $62 per barrel and the forward curve is between $65 and $75. Therefore it is not unreasonable for the North Sea to set out its stall at being sustainable in a $60 world."

A Scottish national oil corporation

There is another factor that is missed by Scots: we don't own a drop of the stuff, and will not do so even if we are independent, unless we take steps to do so. Scotland, or as things stand now, the UK, is unusual in not having a national oil corporation engaged in production and the regulation of the oilfields.

Creating a national oil corporation, from the expertise core represented by the new Oil and Gas Authority, would make Scotland normal, because most other major national oil producer countries have their own company operating in its own oilfields. I am not suggesting we nationalise the North Sea. We as a nation, as I have explained, know so little about the industry that such a step is not feasible. We shall have to live with the variety of companies, large and small, operating there now.

But that does not mean no role for Scottish public interest. Creating our own national oil corporation, which can insist on being a partner in certain fields under production, can secure a partnership of 20% in future licences (Denmark does that), and take part on its own in exploration and production. That would be a start to the ownership participation that we now lack.

Creating a national oil corporation is not rocket science. There are plenty of models around. Norway's Statoil is a public-private partnership. The Norwegian government holds 67% of the company. Setting up a Scottish corporation with, say, a 60-40 split in favour of the public, would attract private investment. The important consequence of creating our own corporation is that, through it, the nation would have a window into this industry, and one of its remits should be to spread knowledge of the industry, so that never again would we be in a state of ignorance, and therefore easy to rob blind.

We have to ask ourselves how a country with vast reserves of energy can be made to believe it is a basket case relying on subsidies from the English? The Yes movement has a great educational task ahead of it. It should be undertaken now.

With all the research resources now available through having fifty-six Westminster MPs (who will have substantial Short money at their disposal) and sixty-four MSPs who themselves have research money available, the SNP is well placed to start and carry out among the public an "oil education campaign" over the next two years. If it does not do so, perhaps Academics for Yes will see a role here.

Scotland has more than oil

Scotland does not have an energy policy. What we have instead is a delusional mess. The target set by the Scottish government of 100% renewables by 2020, just five years away, is the delusion, and the mess is due to a series of muddled policies visited upon us by the powers that be at Westminster, bending to the pressures from the green lobby, combined with the private ownership of the big energy providers whose interests are not the same as the nation's.

In *Why Holyrood Should Control Scotland's Energy Policy*, Nick Dekker, formerly of Strathclyde University and a man with a lifetimes' experience studying the energy industry, opened with: "Energy policy was hardly discussed during the Referendum. Indeed even in the Smith Report it did not seem to register. This is a strange omission when one considers the energy situation Scotland finds itself in, i.e. Scotland is a low-population, energy rich country (oil, gas, wind, hydro, marine) but we are joined to a neighbour with a very different population size, population density, and energy resource situation." In short, Scotland and the UK have different interests in the area of energy.

His paper draws attention to the fact that in respect of the grid our "1,500 MW of hydro and 800 MW of pumped storage assets are a massive technical advantage when operating an electricity grid; especially a grid the size of Scotland's with a peak Scottish electricity demand of around 5,500 MW." He explained that the technical advantage lies in dealing with the consequences of relying more and more on wind generated energy. Those who operate the grid need to guarantee a steady supply to homes and business. As wind turbines, as well as standing idle, can produce excess power at a time when it is not needed, the combination of hydro and pump storage is the technical answer.

Wind is cheap, but not the mechanics of harnessing it. There is nothing wrong with subsidising a new technology in its early stages of operations, but the belief in the "magic" of wind and a policy of substantial subsidy needs looked at with a stern eye.

Wind turbines do not always produce electricity. If there is no wind obviously they produce nothing. That is the case also if the wind is too strong. The result is that each turbine can never reach capacity, the figure so often quoted in those TV reports about lighting up a town. Its actual annual production level is around 28-30% of nominal capacity. I am not suggesting that wind is not a valuable source, but it is difficult to see just how Scottish business and people in their homes have gained a benefit from it under present policies.

The subsidies to wind farms, 100% per turbine, and the cash paid over twenty-five years to rich landowners on whose land the turbines sit, is paid for by higher electricity costs imposed on UK consumers. While 940,000 Scottish households are in fuel poverty, this subsidy system produces the bizarre situation of the Earl of Glasgow being paid £5.525 million over the lifetime of the turbines on his land. The Earl of Seafield will get £3 million, the Earl of Moray £7.5 million and Sir Alastair Gordon-Cumming £10.874 million.

As for production jobs, although Scotland is reputed to have more wind farm capacity per head than any other country, we did not build a single one of the over two thousand wind turbines now installed and operating. Where we should ask, with present policies, lies the benefit from being so energy rich?

That 2020 commitment to full generation from renewables is a self-constructed trap that will be used against the Yes movement in the next referendum, if we do not sort out the mess. To achieve that target with renewables, Scotland will have to produce twice as much electricity as we use. That sounds ridiculous, but as Dekker explains: "If in 2020 we are producing 100% of our own internal demand from renewables, mainly wind and hydro, … we shall still have conventional nuclear and fossil-fuel plants … Hunterston and Torness and the gas plant at Peterhead."

As these nuclear and gas plants are needed to provide a secure baseload when the wind does not blow, and even when it does blow, we shall have a surplus that must be either put through pump storage or exported. That "wind-blown energy" is based on massive subsidy, presently paid by consumers UK-wide, hence the trap. Westminster will taunt us with the absurdity of believing that the rUK consumers will continue to pay those subsidies for Scottish renewables when we are independent, and point out that the whole load of them will be transferred to Scotland, making our electricity costs even higher than at present.

Dekker points to something that is overlooked in the debate about electricity generation. The conventional and hydro-generating plants, now in the hands of private companies, were built by statutory boards SSEB and NSHEB, with public money. They are now in the hands of two companies whose decisions are vital to our economy, but over whom we have no control. That is an unacceptable situation. If Scotland is to be independent, in the full sense of that word, the public must have control of its energy. That does not necessarily mean nationalisation of the present companies, but at least ownership of 51% of each company as the minimum. After all when Scottish assets, built by public money, were sold off, the companies got a bargain from which they have reaped profit ever since. They have had a good run for our money, and cannot complain if their golden days are brought to an end.

In the next referendum as with oil, the Yes movement will have to be better prepared to rebut the scaremongering on energy, and not only make sure it does become a major issue, but is one that we dominate through having the necessary knowledge.

Decommissioning oil rigs
Another bonanza to be missed?

UK Oil & Gas estimates that £10.3 billion worth of decommissioning work will be required in the next ten years, and £28.7 billion will be the total by 2040. Where will the rigs be decommissioned, with thousands of jobs attached to that activity?

Nothing much was made of this job-creating work during the referendum, yet both in terms of the jobs created and the tax take from those in the jobs, it is of enormous potential value. It is estimated that 475 installations, 10,000 km of pipelines, 15 onshore terminals and 5,000 wells will need to be decommissioned over the decades to come. There will be thousands of jobs offshore and onshore involved, not just for a few years but well into 2040 and beyond. These will be skilled jobs, and the decommissioning industry will be creating new technologies and systems that can be "sold" to other oil-producing areas where decommissioning will happen.

This is a jobs bonanza, and an opportunity to raise the levels of skill in our workforce, the level of wages, and give real apprenticeships to our young. It will also open opportunities for our universities engaged in the oil industry to push out new frontiers of knowledge that, again, will enhance the industry's ability to sell abroad.

In the 1970s Scotland missed the chance to make its people live in a full-employment society, with good wages. It would border on criminality to miss out on this opportunity again. That is something the Yes movement should start talking to the people about now.

Better Together claim No.10: the banks & big business will shed jobs

The banks and big business weighed in against the Yes side during the referendum. With some eighteen months between a Yes result and any final creation of an independent Scotland, there was plenty of time for the banks and the supermarkets to gauge the result of negotiations, and take any steps they thought necessary to place themselves in the new context of independence.

They did not take that prudent step. The RBS announcement that it was re-registering its head office in London was conveyed by a hostile media to mean it was closing its main operations in Scotland. If those at the head of RBS were unaware of how this would be presented, then they take the biscuit for naivety. From a Better Together viewpoint the announcement was perfect, further increasing the uncertainty they were pedalling. We can anticipate more of the same from the banks and other sections of the financial sector next time. Standard Life, after the sweeping SNP victory in 2015, has already come out with an attack on independence.

Why anyone should regard the banks as sources of economic wisdom and sensible comment is hard to fathom. The gloom they manufactured at the prospect of independence was more than matched by the hubris that gripped them as they engaged in one of the greatest lending sprees in history, and plunged the Western world into a deep recession. These were the men and women, along with the central bankers, who styled themselves "lords of finance" and "titans of economics", when in fact they were just plain idiotic. Lately many have been found to be just plain criminal, fixing the LIBOR rate to make billions and the Foreign Exchange Market to repeat the fraud. Given the enormous scale of the damage they have done to millions of people through the frauds they have committed, a large number of them should be in jail rather than continuing to draw their bonuses.

We have been constantly told by those at bank boardroom level that they must pay those bonuses, must pay those extravagant salaries, way above anything that the man or woman behind the retail counter get, in order to compete with others worldwide for "talent".

That is one canard we can put aside. If those who ran the financial system into chaos are the best that could be bought, then that best is far from good enough. One only had to look at the inept performance of Rona Fairhead, a director of HSBC (and chair of the BBC Trust), in front of the House of Commons Public Accounts Committee to see the quality that is conspicuous by its absence. She was told by the chair of the committee, "You are either incredibly naive or totally incompetent."

Money, money, money, the bankers' drug

It will be necessary as part of a statement of principles that the Yes movement tackle the issue of the banks. For this to be done, the people must first know what banks are supposed to be for, what practices they engage in, how they can be a threat to our economic stability. They are vulnerable to people gaining knowledge, and wide open to attack given their recent history of criminality.

We all have bank notes in our purses and pockets. It is fiat currency. The link to a fixed point of universal value was abandoned when the United States came off the gold standard in 1972. From then until now, everywhere, in every country, it is fiat currency, that is paper printed by central banks that has no intrinsic value, but which holds a value of exchange because the people using it, nationally and for trading purposes, have confidence in it. If that confidence disappears, the thing we call money simply becomes worthless paper. No one today, for example, would trade a £20 note for a trillion Zimbabwe dollars.

In a world of fiat money, with central banks venturing into the unknown through quantitative easing – printing vast quantities of it electronically, that then sloshes around the world tempting madcap investment – how our banks conduct themselves becomes vital to maintaining economic stability. The present structures are unsafe. To be made safe for society, they need to be divided between "safe banks" and "risky banks", with the former playing a sensible banker role in society, paying attention to retail responsibilities and assisting legitimate business to expand, leaving the latter in the casino fields where, if they fail, then they fail.

The bankers, record is not just poor, but abysmal. They have been proved to be engaged in crooked dealings, which are only matched by a startling level of incompetence.

Between now and the next referendum, the Yes movement has to decide whether an independent Scotland should place itself in a position where the banks can be irresponsible rogues at any time, or whether they are held to another discipline based on restructuring.

Next time we should be prepared, not to retreat when the bankers come in on the side of Unionism, but to counter-attack with the truth about a tribe that deserves public doubt of every word they say, and face them with a policy that makes them the servant not the master of the economy.

Let them debate

To avoid bankers and Scottish Financial Enterprise, the voice of the financial sector, and any of its constituent parts blasting Yes from on high and then retreating into their offices, we need to put them on a hook and keep them there.

The way to do that is set up a series of debates with CEOs of the banks and financial institutions, in Edinburgh and Glasgow, our main financial centres, and demand that the broadcasting authorities enable the people to see how our Lords of Finance stand up to serious scrutiny in the hands of Yes specialists, of whom we have plenty. If STV and BBC will not cooperate then we have enough technical skill in our movement to ensure a very large audience via an alternative media.

Better Together Claim No. 11: Supermarkets will put up their prices

At a key time in the referendum, David Cameron met the supermarket CEOs in Downing Street. He did so individually to avoid any possible breach of company law involving allegations of a cartel. From that meeting we had them state that our shopping trolley prices would rise as a consequence of independence.

The biased media was delighted, and broadcast these statements as if they were based on solid analysis. As for the Unionist Labour Party, we saw Johann Lamont, then leader, photographed outside ASDA celebrating the threat to put up the cost of living for Scots. It is the "distribution" costs, said the supermarkets. Not a single question was posed by reporters about how they justified that claim. Was it based on a careful analysis of where their purchasing came from, including Scottish producers, and where warehouses supplying Scotland are located? Why did Lidl and Aldi not join in the alarm about prices?

Next time, the Yes campaign should put together a group with knowledge of the supermarkets and their operations, and again we have them, a number from Academics for Yes for example, who will seek personal meetings with each of the CEOs to discuss and request information as to why they would find Scotland such a difficult market on independence. We can get our retaliation in first.

Near the end of the referendum, as big business and big oil intervened day and daily, subverting our democratic process, a coordinated part of Project Fear, I issued a statement which brought the *Daily Mail* and others of its type down on my head, and earned me a phone call from Alex Salmond, highly critical of what I had said.

I have reflected upon that statement, and publish it in full below. It was regarded as a mistake by many in the Yes campaign, and I take full responsibility for it. However I think the defensive way it was repudiated by some on our side was an indication of how unprepared the Yes movement was to tackle companies that were then illegitimately in cahoots with a Tory prime minister bent on instilling fear in people:

Issued on 12 September – The No campaign fearmongers have had an effect on me – instead of retiring on 19 September, I am staying in. This referendum is about power, and when we get a Yes majority, we will use that power for a day of reckoning with BP and the banks.

The heads of those companies are rich men in cahoots with a rich English Tory prime minister to keep Scotland poor, poorer through lies and distortions. The power they have now to subvert our democracy will come to an end with Yes.

BP, in an independent Scotland, will need to learn the meaning of nationalisation, in part or in whole, as it has in other countries who have not been as soft as we have been forced to be. If it wants into the "monster fields" in the areas west of Shetland, it will have to learn to bend the knee to a greater power – us, the sovereign people of Scotland. We will be the masters of the oil fields, not BP or any other of the majors. If Bob Dudley thinks this is mere rhetoric, just let him wait. It is sovereign power that counts. We will have it, he will not.

As for the Bankers. Your casino days, rescued by socialisation of your liabilities while you waltz off with the profits, will be over. You will be split between retail and investment, and if your greed takes the latter down, there will be no rescue. You believe in the market, in the future you will live with its discipline. Fall will mean failure.

As for Standard Life, it will be required by new employment laws to give two years warning of any redundancies, and reveal to the trade unions its financial reasons for relocation to any country outside of Scotland, and the costs involved. It has never crossed the minds of our compliant Unionist media, especially the BBC, to ask the chief executive what his costs are on his proposed moves.

As for John Lewis, the question is whether the senior management consulted the "partners" or took instructions from Cameron? Another question our supine BBC did not ask. There is now talk of boycott, and if it happens, it will be a management own goal.

What kind of people do these companies think we are? They will find out.

Dealing with the best pals of
Better Together
The media

There were demonstrations against the public service broadcaster, the BBC, for its bias towards Better Together. The criticism was justified. If anyone doubts that, then they should read G.A. Ponsonby's book *London Calling: How the BBC stole the Referendum*. Better Together and the Labour Party campaigns were notable for their closed meetings, i.e. a picked audience. You would never have known that from the way these meetings were broadcast, by comparison with the non-broadcast of the Yes open meetings, with hundreds attending. The way Alex Salmond was depicted on BBC by Nick Robinson's claim that Alex had failed to answer his questions was revealed to be a straight lie by the social media which broadcast the whole press conference. That is not due to carelessness. It was deliberate.

When I was interviewed on BBC News, the presenter laid in front of me all the propaganda that had poured on our heads from Better Together as though it was gospel.

The smearing of Alex Salmond

I and others could not put our finger on why it was necessary for some speakers to say "The referendum is not about Alex Salmond and the White Paper" or why reports came in that he was not popular with women. I have my differences with Alex, over policies, but he is pleasant with people, good company, likes a joke, is honest and is a master of debate. So, where did this distrust come from? Ponsonby's book tells why. From the time he became First Minister in 2007, the BBC ran a systematic smear campaign against him. *London Calling* gives page after page of evidence against the BBC. It cites what for me was one of the worst episodes on 24 November 2010: "In the clip shown on Reporting Scotland, the camera initially focused on the Finance Secretary who was heard to say: 'I express my regret to the parliament that in retrospect I clearly did not get those judgements correct.' The video then immediately cut away to Mr Salmond who was shown shaking his head in an almost flippant manner whilst feigning a nonchalant 'ooohhh' in mock concern. The camera then cut back to an apparently forlorn looking Finance Secretary. To most casual viewers it appeared as though the First Minister hadn't treated the apology seriously" (p. 79).

However, the official Holyrood video from which the BBC took the clip showed Alex sitting in respectful silence as John Swinney read out his statement – no shaking head, and no movement of the lips. His head shaking and verbal mocking sound came later in that session in response to an attack from Tavish Scott of the Lib Dems. How could a video be so spliced in a way that showed Alex Salmond in a bad light? Accidently? Not when you read that this was only one of many, many occasions when Salmond was traduced, while BBC Scotland acted as a mouthpiece for Better Together.

Can we expect better?

I doubt if BBC Scotland and BBC in London can be different next time. Only a few journalists emerge from Ponsonby's evisceration with credit: James Cook, Isobel Fraser, David Miller and Ken Macdonald. The problem is that unlike the other media outlets, it can be immune to criticism, because of the poll tax basis of the licence fee. Were the licence fee to be decriminalised, it would be possible to organise a mass "can pay won't pay" campaign that defeated that other poll tax. Perhaps, ironically, the Tory government, with its own complaints against the BBC, may decriminalise non-payment of the TV licence, and enable that tactic to come into play in future.

Scotland's other media, television, radio and newspapers are private companies. That does not mean they are immune from the public mood. Commercial media are in a marketplace where they must sell their products, and that means they cannot ignore the views of their readers and viewers. The position of the *Daily Record* is interesting. The *Record* has a long history of backing Labour in whatever it says or does. In March 2014, along with Peter Kearney, I met the editor and deputy editor. They explained that while about a third of their readers favoured independence the majority did not. We told them that something was happening below the media radar, and that by August, that readership position would have changed. We repeated that message to the editor and deputy editor of the *Herald*. As the campaign progressed, while the *Record* certainly leant in favour of No, the Yes side case got a good amount of space. Due to its contact with its readers, the *Record* caught the changes taking place and, no doubt to the frustration of the Labour leadership, the *Record* did not come out for No. The *Herald* too was more balanced than, for example, the *Scotsman*, which became a hopeless case with falling circulation. There is strange chemistry that unites a newspaper and its readers, and a good editor picks up what they are thinking. *It is possible therefore to influence how the printed press seeks to influence the campaign. Letters to the editor are all read even if not all printed, and phone calls when a paper's journalist is not simply critical, but outrageously unfair and poisonous, do have an effect.*

The other Good Pals of Better Together: the Institute for Fiscal Studies and the Office for Budget Responsibility

Next time, as last time, the Yes campaign will face the claims of the Office for Budget Responsibility, the Institute for Fiscal Studies and other think tanks, telling us how independence will beggar the country. These will be given great prominence in the Unionist media, as the OBR and IFS are described as "authoritative" and above political suspicion. Take those claims with a bucket of salt.

The OBR is a UK Government organisation, set up by the Budget Responsibility and National Audit Act 2011. Three members of its lead committee are appointed by the Chancellor of the Exchequer. At present they are Robert Chote, chairman, former director of the IFS, Stephen Nickell CBE, member of the Bank of England Monetary Policy Committee for six years, and Graham Parker CBE, a former treasury official. Its Oversight Board is those three plus Lord Burns, former permanent sectary at the Treasury for seven years, and Dame Kate Barker CBE, a former member of the Bank of England Monetary Policy Committee for nine years, and formerly chief economic adviser to the CBI. There is an Advisory Panel on which people from the Bank of England, academia and other bodies sit. Not exactly free from entanglement with the government and the metropolitan financial establishment.

Those intimate links to the UK government should make Scots cautious about accepting OBR forecasting the consequences of independence. It is hardly an independent body given that it is funded by the Treasury, appointed by the chancellor, and can be dismissed by him with the agreement of the Treasury Select Committee.

On 13 June 2015, the *Scotsman* so believed a forecast by the OBR of "a dramatic fall in North Sea oil revenues over the next 25 years" that it gave pride of place to it in its leader column. In a letter to the paper, describing the leader as hitting a new level of absurdity, I pointed out:

Forecasting the direction of the price of any basic commodity over the next 25 years requires a total understanding of the global economy, and society, not now, but in the future. Here are, among others, some of the things a forecaster needs to know for certain – the consequences on its growth of China shifting to another economic model, will the Eurozone continue to see the triumph of politics over economics, how will QE be unwound in the short or long term, how will Japan escape – if ever – from stagnation, whether the USA is in relative decline, what effect will Modi's policies have on India in the long term, will the Philippines and Vietnam continue on a growth path, what effect will Indonesian politics have on its economic performance, will Africa develop its full potential, when will recessions occur and how deep they will be, not to mention wars and rumours of wars as states in Asia jockey for position.

All that has to be understood and assessed in any forecast about oil. That you should believe the OBR capable of such brilliant, indeed unique analysis, shows you are, in a big way, subject to the wish being father to the thought. Twenty-five years? The OBR record shows it is pretty useless at forecasting much shorter and more measurable time scales. Its forecast for UK economic growth between 2010 to mid 2012 was 5.7%, whereas it was 0.9%. Its forecast for 2012 was 2.8% growth, and it was 0.3%. For business investment its forecast was 10% for 2012, and it was 0.4%.

With a record of spectacular errors, why should the Scots accept what it says about independence? *Between now and next time, we have to expose the OBR to Scots as a deeply flawed, UK government organisation we should ignore.*

The Institute for Fiscal Studies

The IFS describes itself as "an independent research institute" and has been described by the *Daily Telegraph* as the "most respected economic forecaster" and by the *Guardian* as a "respected think tank". So right across the political spectrum we have adulation. We Scots, as with the OBR, should again be more sceptical in accepting IFS at its self-proclaimed face value. When it comes to slicing and dicing a Westminster budget, the IFS will be objective. When, however, as part of the UK establishment, whether it is willing to admit it or not, it is on the Unionist side on the issue of Scottish independence.

"Scotland's deficit higher in first year of independence than UK's, says IFS" was a good example of the newspaper headlines on 4 June 2014, reporting a study timed nicely for the referendum and Unionist propaganda. Severin Carrell, Scottish correspondent of the *Guardian*, reported that IFS based its analysis on, yes, you've guessed it, the Office for Budget Responsibility data. A nice nexus of Establishment interest.

The IFS, as part of the Metropolitan elite, is about as neutral on Scottish independence as the Duke of Buccleuch. The mistake made by the IFS is that it has no conception of how Scots could run their country differently from the failed model, which manages to deliver poverty to one million out of five million. It may be a think tank, but it doesn't think deep enough, or understand enough the alternatives to what it measures and comments upon, which is a Unionist

Scotland as a North British bit of the UK economy. We should be less solicitous next time with the IFS and others like it. Any outfit which considers data from the OBR to be valid should have its opinion treated with scepticism.

What Yes did not successfully get cross, despite some excellent work by groups, was that we're not talking of independence as a means to create a Scottish state that would be a mini UK, but a very different one in its economic structures and the moral nature of our society, with the aim of correcting the gross inequalities that now mark us to our shame. That is beyond the mind and understanding of the IFS, anchored as it is in the South East region. There is more on this in Part II.

Better Together Claim No. 12: The Vow

What was the Vow? Just the statement made by the then three leaders of the Tory, Lib Dem and Labour parties? Or was the Gordon Brown speech in the Miners Welfare Club in Loanhead part of it? The answer to that is important. The BBC and others in the media made much of what Brown had to say, bandying around words like "quasi-federalism" and "Devo max". Given the importance of the Labour vote it is fair to say that Brown's intervention, and his assertions, as I shall show, were as important as the statement from the other three.

Here is the full text of the official Vow printed in the *Daily Record*:

The people of Scotland will want to know that all three main parties will deliver change for Scotland.

We are agreed that:

The Scottish Parliament is permanent and extensive new powers for the Parliament will be delivered by the process and to the timetable agreed and announced by our three parties, starting on 19th September.

And it is our hope that the people of Scotland will be engaged directly as each party works to improve the way we are governed in the UK in the years ahead.

We agree that the UK exists to ensure opportunity and security for all by sharing our resources equitably across all four nations to secure the defence, prosperity and welfare of every citizen.

And because of the continuation of the Barnett allocation for resources, and the powers of the Scottish Parliament to raise revenue, we can state categorically that the final say on how much is spent on the NHS will be a matter for the Scottish Parliament.

We believe that the arguments that so powerfully make the case for staying together in the UK should underpin our future as a country. We will honour those principles and values not only before the referendum but after.

People want to see change. A No vote will deliver faster, safer and better change than separation.

Most of the above is verbiage, with the exception of "extensive new powers" and "continuation of the Barnett allocation for resources". What was meant by "extensive new powers" was not, however, spelled out. That was not the case with Gordon Brown. On 8 September he set out twelve policy areas, including powers to create a non-profit-making railway company and housing benefit, with the latter meaning, as he declared, "There never again could be a bedroom tax imposed by Westminster on Scotland."

Were they part of the Vow? In his letter to Lord Smith on 30 September, Brown said he was passing him "the documents that I had assembled from my pre-referendum talks with the pro-devolution political parties about the timetable for further devolution and the signing of the vow."

Coming into the final stages of the campaign, the BBC reported, "It is understood the three main Westminster parties will formally back Mr Brown's proposals on Tuesday," with the Vow. Removing any doubt, the BBC quoted a Downing Street source saying about the Brown position, "This is in line with the fruits of the cross-party discussions." So we can take what was said in the vague Vow and put flesh on that skeleton by including in it what Brown had to say. He was never corrected by Better Together or the Westminster parties, which were all happy to see his speeches and statements lapped up and transmitted by the BBC and *Daily Record*.

Was the Vow of no importance?

Unionists have insisted, and are backed by post-referendum research, that the Vow was not crucial to the result. One statistic quoted is that it made only a 3.4% difference in favour of the No vote. Statistics take no account of the politics.

Had that 3.4% been added to the 44.7%, Yes, we would have had 48.1&, and the No vote reduced to

51.9%. In political terms the narrower the vote, the better for the Yes side, because the gap next time will be seen as much more easy to overcome. There is another political dimension which the research cannot, I suggest, actually measure. In a referendum obviously the Yes and No votes count, but so in a way do abstentions; no one knows just how effective the Vow was in persuading Labour voters in Glasgow and Dundee, unhappy with their party's position but uncomfortable about voting against it, to abstain (both were relatively lower turnout areas compared with the rest of Scotland).

The main political fact is that the Vow was made, and it is against the Gordon Brown policies at the heart of the Vow that the new devolved powers will be judged, and also against the powers that independence would have brought.

The reality of the Vow – a trap and a Veto

The Westminster government appointed the Smith Commission to hazard a guess at what the Vow was, which of course was an admission that when it was made the three who signed it did not know what it meant. Smith brought in five parties: Labour, Tory, Lib Dems (all Unionist), the SNP and the Greens. Yes Scotland advisory board, the Scottish Socialist Party, RIC, Women for Independence, Academics for Independence, and others who played a prominent role in the Yes campaign were not invited. Why the SNP joined in that restricted group chaired by a Unionist, where they were outnumbered and would be required to compromise with the majority, is something only the leadership can explain. Did they have no red lines? The word "extensive" gave them plenty of room to demand a lot, and sign a minority report if they did not get it.

The outcome was the Smith report recommendations, and following it a Command Paper 8990, issued by the Westminster government, setting out the further powers to be devolved, and now the Scotland Bill. The SNP 2015 election manifesto stated, "We will demand, firstly, that the proposals of the Smith Commission are delivered quickly and in full. We believe that these proposals do not go far enough to honour the promises made during the referendum. We will seek agreement that the Scottish Parliament should move to full financial responsibility."

That extract from the manifesto is a good example of the lack of intellectual rigour. As no one knew exactly what the Vow of more "extensive powers" meant, by what alchemy did the SNP know the Smith Commission did not meet it? When the Smith Commission reported, why did the SNP sign up to it, knowing the powers it proposed did not meet the Vow?

The one club in the bag policy

We should all be indebted to the Jimmy Reid Foundation for the paper, *Smith Commission: why the economic and fiscal arrangements need to be changed,* authored by Jim and Margaret Cuthbert. The Cuthberts could never be accused of lacking intellectual rigour. Their paper demonstrates that the government plan to implement

Smith is not more extensive and significant powers for Holyrood, but a devolution trap which, if implemented, would prevent growth and prevent a real attack on inequality.

There is only one major tax, one club in the bag, to be transferred to Holyrood – income tax. But not all income tax. Income earned through savings, and income that comes from dividends is excluded. If privately owned business decided to pay itself in dividends instead of salaries, then the take from income tax comes down.

In their paper the Cuthberts lay bare the folly of accepting and relying upon that single tax.

The various "taxable earnings bands" in Scotland show the true nature of the flaw in using only income tax. Ours is a low-income nation, and the national average wage is lower than for the rest of the UK. That matters, but what also matters is our position in the earnings bands of £50,000 and above, and the yield of income tax they can bring.

The Cuthberts point out, "There are marked differences in the tax base between Scotland and the rest of the UK. These principally relate to the fact that Scotland has proportionately far fewer taxpayers with earnings at the upper end of the income scale. … Scotland has 8.3% of the UK population. … for income bands from £50,000 up, the Scottish share of UK income tax falls progressively below Scotland's population share, dropping to 3.77% for the income band of over £200,000 (HMRC, based on liabilities)."

The Cuthberts identify a wheeze, that we shall be assigned 50% of VAT income raised in Scotland. That too is flawed as assessment of VAT from Scotland is far from precise, more like a guesstimate. But anyway, what we might gain from that, we shall lose on the block grant coming from Westminster via the Barnett formula, which itself will be subject to adjustments – post-Smith at least 50% of Holyrood's income will be controlled from Westminster.

Getting done the Greek way?
Or paddling around in the mud of devolution

As the Cuthberts note, "any Scottish government will actually be severely constrained in its freedom of action. … The perversity of the way the Smith reforms are being implemented means that Scotland could well find itself in a position rather like Greece – locked into a cycle of relative decline within a malfunctioning monetary union. Indeed in certain important respects, Scotland's position would be worse than that of Greece. Scotland is a resource rich country, but barred from controlling or accessing much of its own resources, and Scotland does not have anything like the range of economic and taxation powers possessed by Greece."

Why the independence movement has to paddle around in the mud of devolution, diverting its strength and attention in trying to make the unworkable work, might seem a mystery. Put it down to the long learnt skill of the Whitehall establishment in sucking the life out of a political force that threatens its hegemony.

We did not make enough of a written constitution

The SNP government published a paper on a written constitution during the referendum, but it did not have much impact, which was a pity. In the meetings I spoke at the question of the monarchy or a republic was raised time and again, but strictly on those terms, and not in the wider context of a written constitution. Perhaps others had a better experience.

I said a "pity" because the benefit of a written constitution was one of the reasons why Yes should have won. Maybe when seen against the issues of currency, economy, EU, NATO, Trident, oil, shipbuilding, security, a constitution was regarded as of secondary importance. But the power it gives to the individual citizen should mark it out as equally important.

A written constitution, justiciable in the courts, allows the individual citizen, groups of citizens, communities, civic organisations and companies to challenge the executive acts and laws of government, and have them annulled if those acts and laws are contrary to the powers given to a parliament by a constitution.

Westminster constitutional theory is that Parliament is sovereign and, not withstanding membership of the European Union, that remains the case as the English Lord Chief Justice made clear in a speech earlier in the year. There are no constraints on politicians in government. That is where a written constitution is different. It defines the boundaries that constrain governments, and carries the ability, through the courts, to challenge and have struck down any non-constitutional act or Act a government brings forward.

The Yes campaign, next time, must build a better understanding that independence with a written constitution is something of great value to the individual citizen, the foundation of a true state of civil liberty. Yes groups could start discussing it now.

The current state of play

In this part of the book I have sought to delve into the claims that Better Together made, and subject them to a deeper analysis than proved possible for the Yes side during the campaign itself.

Throughout I have written about the next time. The next time is not something the Yes movement should sit and wait for. Next time is something the Yes movement has to bring forward, by continued campaigning and activity.

It has been said that one major result of the referendum is that the people in Scotland are now better politically educated than any former generation. I am not sure that is true, but it is certainly true by comparison with the past thirty years, during which the Labour Party abandoned political education as an essential part of what Harold Wilson called its "crusade", and the trade union movement declined in numbers and influence.

But unless the Yes movement maintains its effort to engage people in meetings, seminars, lectures and discussion groups, and provides well researched information, our nation will slip back. That thirst for knowledge is there; it is the task of the independence movement to meet that need. *We must always remember that knowledge is power.*

PART II

Issues that will have a bearing on next time
The role of political parties

Next time can only arrive when a political party, on its own or together with other parties, seeks and gets a majority in the Holyrood Parliament for independence and a referendum to deliver it. The SNP was the instrument that brought us the referendum last September, and it will be a political party that brings us the next one.

The mandate can only be obtained in the context of a Holyrood election, as only in that forum is Scotland alone involved in an election decision. David Cameron's announcement soon after the Westminster result that there would be no referendum for a generation, betrayed a colonial attitude that failed to understand the forces let loose in 2014. It will not be possible for him or any successor to ignore a democratic decision for an independence mandate and a referendum.

What are the prospects for 2016? Will the SNP seek a mandate for independence, or will it play safe and campaign on its record in government, and how it has showed a willingness to work constructively with the other parts of the UK? What is the SNP priority? Is it to preserve its majority in Holyrood, continue with the strategy of building confidence in its competence as a government so that, at some future time, not defined, people will take its advice and vote Yes for independence?

That would be a continuation of the strategy pursued

previously, which was successful in that the party got into government, and then subsequently won a majority. But it was not successful in winning an independence vote. We shall not know until the SNP manifesto is published in 2016 whether it will "play safe for a majority" or put itself and its seats on the line for an independence mandate. Perhaps we will get a clue from the temper of the 2015 annual conference, when the new membership's influence will start to tell, or not.

Although apparently completely dominant following the fifty-six out of fifty-nine seats won in May 2015, the SNP is not the only party in our politics. Holyrood will be fought on proportional representation, opening the doors to others who may put independence at the top of the agenda.

At the time of writing, it appears that a New Left grouping is being formed, of people who appear to see no real chance of creating a very different Scotland without the powers of independent government. If by Christmas 2015 it has gained the necessary organisational strength through which to raise finance, and put candidates in the field next May, the SNP will find itself outflanked on the Left, and under pressure on the issue of campaigning unambiguously for independence, however strange that might seem. But putting the non-Labour Left together with an agreed policy platform that people will believe is realistic, and will vote for, is, as socialist history shows, no easy task.

How does Scotland create a more effective economy? The role of resource management

What we have, due to our integration with the UK, is a low wage, high unemployment, high poverty level economy. Outside of every Lidl supermarket in Scotland is a sign saying that one in four Scottish children lives in poverty. I have already mentioned the one million out of five million in the same boat. In the UK we face more austerity and possibly, probably, another recession. That is the economy we shall inherit, and the one we shall have to rebuild with independence.

Independence is the way out of that mess. This is something the Institute for Fiscal Studies and others of that ilk never could grasp. Independence offers the opportunity to pursue a different economic policy based on an economic model different from being simply a northern bit of the UK economy.

We have to look at two things: demand and resource management. The UK pursues the classic Keynesian path of overcoming problems by boosting demand in the economy for goods and services. The accumulation of purchases by an English-Welsh population of fifty-four million is a considerable market in which "demand" plays a significant role. The national debt and private debt levels, at astronomical levels, have been the means of maintaining demand and boosting it back after the fall in GDP following the financial crisis.

Scotland as a trading nation will be affected by demand in our largest market, the rUK, in Europe and elsewhere. We cannot escape that fact. As for domestic demand in Scotland, even with the growth of population it will be only one of the drivers of economic performance; ours is a small fractured market: populations of 3,000,000 in the central belt, 780,000 in subregions of Grampian, 148,000 in Dumfries and Galloway, 256,000 in the Highlands and Islands, and 112,000 in the Borders.

But we cannot submit ourselves to having our economic policy being dominated by the level of demand in other countries. This is where resource management comes in. Against that global demand influence, we need to balance it with greater prominence given to resource management. That relies upon an identification of indigenous assets, from which products and services can be created, and traded internally and internationally. Policies aimed at building on our resources will provide a robust pillar to the economy. Scotland's resources can be identified as

(1) People
(2) Education system
(3) Potential in energy generation
(4) Land and agriculture
(5) Fisheries
(6) Oil
(7) Cities
(8) Scenery
(9) Topography
(10) Geography
(11) Heritage
(12) Water
(13) Whisky
(14) Food & Drink

People are our greatest resource. Their education the most important function of government. We are five million in a world of over seven billion people. We are living in an age of great change. World economic power has shifted to Asia-Pacific, a momentous development in itself, but we also face the technological revolution where, unlike previous times, we have no inherent advantage.

The Industrial Revolution being born in the West gave us advantage in that we had experience of managing industries, giving us a level of skill rarely matched by under developed countries. For example, when Saudi Arabia and other Gulf states sought to build modern economies, they had to import American and European management expertise in those early stages. That learnt advantage has not applied anywhere in the technological revolution. Whether in the Middle East or Asia, young generations have taken to mastering it like ducks to water.

To rebuild Scotland in this new world, we must put greater emphasis on education. It is not good enough for us to parrot that we have a world-class one when we do not. We are falling down the OECD rankings when we should be rising. It is from a better educated people that will flow the ideas and activity needed by Scotland in the future. From education flows everything else, not only the maintenance of the economy, but the civilised level of our society, and what we can contribute to humankind.

Just a couple of ideas

If we are to lift our economy to a different level, we need to bring more of our people into the socio-economic mainstream, from which many are excluded now.

That means looking at how to open up regions presently in semi-isolation. It means **roads** that will open up the country. Right now Galloway is isolated. You only need to drive, or take the train to Stranraer to see how isolated. Dumfries region is better placed, but again there are areas of isolation. North Ayrshire is cut off from the main motorway system, and that itself needs upgrading. The A9 road to the Highlands is a good case in point. Our present ambition is to make it, step by step, a dual carriageway, when a full motorway is required. That the West Highlands need for a proper major road system is evident.

Opening up regions makes them more accessible for business to invest in them, and for goods to get from them to markets. Opening up can also give a boost to **tourism**, especially if the idea that I argue for on oil and fuel pricing is taken as an objective. Tourism, which is built on a number of our resources, has to be seen for what it actually is: an "export" in situ, of culture, history, scenery, facilities, services. An improvement in the comprehensive promotion of Scotland, aid to upgrading of hotels and other accommodation, greater emphasis on the professionalism of jobs within the industry, and cheaper fuel costs, is what we can do when independent.

Oil and fuel costs. Ours is a small country with a great deal of oil. We should use some of it to reduce the price of fuel. That policy, an example of resource management, would be good for all businesses, supermarkets, shops, transport, airlines using our airports, the family budget, and a huge boost to tourism.

It would be worthwhile Left parties considering just how economic activity can be built on our entire indigenous resource base, and so preparing to put a comprehensive economic plan to the people next time we need to win a referendum.

Final economic word – the benefits of being small

There are economic advantages for both large states and small ones, as can be seen from the respective performances of Germany (80 million), Norway (4.7 million), Denmark (5 million) and Singapore (5 million).

The standing in world economic league tables shows that the main advantage lies with small states. The reason is that in dealing with policies, a small state can be versatile and nimble; like small ships compared to giant carriers on the ocean, they can turn faster from problems and towards solutions. The alleged disadvantage of an independent Scotland, that it is too small to break away from the UK, is false. That smallness of Scotland accounts for the promptness of its government's communications with every part of it, the easier access to government by people and business, making it easier to correct errors in decision-making.

A smaller state's government can exercise both macroeconomic policy and microeconomic management much more easily than a large state can. Its relationship with business, and its knowledge of what is actually happening on the ground in its communities, far surpass that of a large state.

Can intolerable austerity be tolerated?

We now know that further austerity will be coming from a Tory government which has been rejected in Scotland but has a majority in the House of Commons.

The punishment of the poor is to continue, making them pay the cost of the consequences of a recession they did not bring about.

The confidence with which the Westminster government has launched the new round of welfare cuts is testament to the successful PR campaign that the *Daily Mail* and other Tory papers have been conducting over the past five years. They have been able to scapegoat the poor, because that is not difficult. We do have a very small minority of shysters in our communities, who damage the reputation of the welfare state, but they are dwarfed, it must be said, with the damage done by the shysters in the financial community.

As the shysters in the upper and big business classes prey upon the community largely in anonymity, they can hide behind the "corporate" mask when exposed, as in banking scandals, i.e. it was the bank that fiddled the Forex system, the bank that got fined, few individual names, few prosecutions, no large group of criminals paraded across our TV screens. To the general public these people are unseen, dealing in tricks and rip-offs that are hard to understand.

But take a typical case in a locality, in a housing scheme – a man or woman claiming benefit when they are perfectly fit, or those working the system – what my granny called those "who would not work, nor want." This very small minority who, unlike the crooks in the city, are very visible to the rest of us, are easy to resent. Their conduct is used by the Tories and their allies to smear those who genuinely and honestly rely on help through the welfare state.

Who are the big fraudsters?

The irony is that the contrast between "our" shysters and the rich shysters is vast. According to the government's own figures, the total amount of fraud and error in the welfare benefits system is 1.9% of total spend. Fraud itself accounts for 0.7%, claimant error 0.8%, and errors by officials 0.4%. At the upper end of the shyster group, the financial community, fraud on a gigantic scale was committed in the rigging of the London Interbank Offered Rate. LIBOR serves as the first stage in calculating interest rates on loans made by banks throughout the world, either in overnight deposits, or with one, two, three, six and twelve months to maturity of the loan. There are thirty-five LIBOR rates set in each business day, thus providing great scope for manipulating the rate through fraud, enabling the fraudster, his co-fraudsters and their banks to make illegal billions. At the time of writing, while banks that were caught have paid US$6.5 billion in fines, only one man is standing trial. One man?

Then there are the Forex frauds perpetrated by at least ten banks, including RBS and Barclays, with most of the operators based in London. This is a huge market, trading US$5.3 trillion per day, and was rigged from 2007 until discovered in 2013. So far the fines amount to £6.3 billion. But what about the people defrauded all over the world? Many will never know that they were robbed.

Back to the future

But despite the difference between that tiny minority who defraud the taxpayer and those in the financial sectors who defraud the world on a scale beyond an ordinary person's imagination, it is still easier to rouse public anger and get public support for harsher policies on all the poor.

We have been transported back to the Victorian era: once again we have rich rulers deciding that there are deserving and undeserving poor, and so large a number are the latter that they now "merit" special attention. If in Tory Britain you are poor, you are guilty of the social crime of being poor, and laws will be applied to you in order that you be humiliated, sanctioned, made destitute, driven to food banks and reduced to the status of a serf whose life is in the hands of a bureaucratic state machine.

Warren Buffett, a very rich American, has admitted the truth: that capitalist governments run a welfare state not for the poor, but for coddling the rich. *International Business Times* was outraged by his words and their rebuke revealed the truth, as they knew it was unlikely they would be read in the poorer districts of New York or Glasgow:

> Buffett says that the super-rich generally face a 15 percent tax rate on most of their earnings. But he fails to tell the entire story: The super-rich, because of their vast wealth and resources, are always several steps ahead of the taxman. Private bankers know the drill full well – they stash their

clients' wealth in off-shore tax havens and are always on the lookout for new ways to escape the debilitating effects of taxes on their client's holdings.

Who can blame them? Why should the super-rich – or the middle class, for that matter – be required to cough up an increasingly fatter share of their hard-earned cash to foot the bill for a segment of society that been trained to sit back and expect the state to take care of them?

Now we know. An unabashed admission of financial power by a self-styled elite, combined with contempt for the poor.

Immigration

The weakness of the poor arises from the weakness of all who do not have the gift of inherited wealth. Because of that weakness, we have to sell our labour by hand or brain, in order to earn a living. That lesson was usually learnt the hard way by the working class, but the deluge let loose by the financial crisis washed away ignorance of that fundamental fact among accountants, lawyers, estate agents and other professionals. The middle classes felt the sting of unemployment.

Workers' bargaining power in the labour market has been reduced significantly, hence the spread of zero-hours contracts and jobs that carry no more than the minimum wage. Reconciling this increased bargaining power, which can only be achieved through policies aimed at full employment, and the acceptance of immigration is a conundrum that the Scottish Left must resolve.

The Left in Scotland has not engaged in any in-depth discussion about immigration policy, as distinct from highlighting serious wrongs in the treatment of people. That immigration is high up on the political agenda cannot be ignored, and the sensitive issues that confront the host nation's citizens in responding to immigration and the humanitarian issues involved have to be properly explored.

The economic case for immigration

There is an instinctive psychological barrier to the accept-ance of immigration. It is not wise to ignore it. That in built reticence has to be taken into account when making what is a strong economic case for more immigrants coming to Scotland.

Scotland's population was in long term decline. It fell from 5.24 million in 1974 to 5.06 million in 2000. But that trend has been reversed. It now stands at 5.347 million due, as the Registrar General's report shows, to net immigration over the past eight years. We have an ageing population, and therefore need greater num-bers of young people to earn and pay taxes to fund the social care system needed in the years ahead. Also, an ageing population does not produce children. That is done by the young, and that requires greater numbers of migrants. There is no evading that fact.

A nation that grows in population gets benefits from that growth. At the simplest economic level, there is greater demand for food products, transport, energy, housing, schools, services, and the consequence of that increase in demand is more jobs and higher tax income for government, and as a further consequence more affordable public spending. There are add-ons, such as bringing into our society people with energy, talent and ability, who will contribute to our knowledge, continue to internationalise our higher education, and contribute to innovation in our industries, both manufacturing and services, and so further grow the economy. As for cultural strains, there is great strength in Scotland's culture as was shown by how it resisted efforts when we used to be described as North Britain, to anglicise much of it. Of course living with cultures between a host nation and immigrants is not easy for either party at first, but we in Scotland have a good record of enjoying diversity without losing a sense of common identity.

How open should be the door?

Now we need to come to the difficult detail the Left and the rest of Scottish society has to address. How many immigrants, and how open will the door be to them? The SNP manifesto for 2015 says, "We will support sensible immigration policies that meet our economic needs and, as a priority, we will seek the reintroduction of the post study visa, so that those we have helped educate are able, if they so choose, to make a contribution to our economy."

The SNP did not define "sensible immigration" policy, and so far neither has anyone on the Left. It cannot mean a completely open door, because that would be unacceptable to the present population, and would pose severe problems for national and local government in relation to allocation of resources, and how much resources there would be, for housing, schools and the NHS. The Left believes in planning, and planning for population growth – bringing in new young people who will produce children – demands an answer to how many?

Here we are not talking about asylum seekers. **They must be admitted**. We are talking of two categories of economic migrants: (a) people working outside their countries in order to make money to be sent back to families at home, with themselves intending to return home permanently and (b) those who are seeking to settle permanently in Scotland as a way to a better life.

Different categories?

Are we to look on both migrants as the same, or are we to create different policies for each? It is a valid question containing a number of issues that the Left and the trade union movement must address, because there are serious and different issues posed by both, to the economy and to the strength and capability of trade unions.

Before addressing these matters, Scots, who are among the world's most prolific economic migrants, cannot both boast of how talented Scots migrants have helped build Canada, Australia and New Zealand, without acknowledging that migrants coming to our shores are also of the same high quality, and can make a significant contribution rebuilding our nation. It takes great character to leave your homeland and settle somewhere else, or go to work in a foreign country as an expat. It takes even greater character for people to board an overcrowded decrepit vessel and go off into a dangerous Mediterranean sea.

Economic migrants who come on temporary visits for work, have been shown to be exploited by employers through lower rates of pay, long working hours and have their contracts manipulated to get round EU rules meant to protect them. Their presence in the labour market depresses both job opportunities and wage rates for indigenous workers. Their accommodation can either be overcrowded or otherwise substandard. They put up with these conditions because the main aim is to have the lowest possible living costs here, in order to maximise the money sent home. The chances of getting them to join a trade union are slim.

The situation at Rosyth is a good example of the above. According to Unite, as reported in the media, Eastern European workers recruited by a number of organisations have three-month contracts that require long working hours and, to avoid the EU rule that says after twelve weeks a foreign worker must be paid local rates is met, they are taken back home, and sign a new three-month contract on the original terms and conditions. Business is happy. It has cheap non-unionised labour at its mercy.

Issues that cannot be dodged: temporary EU foreign workers

We cannot dodge the consequences for Scots workers of free movement. Unlike the temporary three-month contractors, they have to pay mortgages, feed, clothe and send their children to school, and seek to give them a good start in life. If jobs disappear, not because they are not there, but because they have been taken by others, then Scots' living standards are threatened.

As we are in the EU, and as free movement of labour is one of its pillars and likely to remain so, no matter what the present government suggests, this issue will remain with us. As many Scots work as foreign workers in the expat sector in many countries, not only the EU, we can hardly complain if others do the same as our relatives. But by expanding the numbers seeking work, and so giving employers the chance to undercut the wages of indigenous workers, free movement has problems to which we have to find a solution.

We can only act when independent

Given that barring EU foreign workers is not legally possible, there is only one way to ensure absolutely that the temporary workers and home Scots are both protected to the best extent possible, and that is through changes to employment law. However, that remains a reserved matter for Westminster, and as with many other policies, we are stuck until we gain independence.

But the power independence would give opens up possibilities to do very different things through employment laws, and we must hope next time trade unions in Scotland, whatever their executive located down south says, will back Yes, because it will be in the interests of their members to do so.

Independent power over employment laws would

enable us to set up an effective registration and monitoring system. Companies recruiting foreign workers to work in Scotland, whether from the EU or elsewhere, would be subject to regulation, conducted by a government-funded authority. All temporary foreign workers would be required to register with the authority, giving information on who recruited them, copies of their contracts, how many contracts they had signed, the wage rates offered, hours to be worked, and details of the accommodation and costs charged against them. Any employer taking on foreign labour not registered would be guilty of a criminal offence. The authority would be able to state what was the "core" wage in an area, and require that rate be paid. The authority proposed would have as its executive chairman a person nominated by the Scottish TUC, with trade unions, the Federation of Small Business and the CBI allocated seats on the board.

Those of the neo-liberal bent will argue that such regulation would insert rigidities in what they believe is *the* essential for growth – a flexible labour market. What they mean is that in their kind of labour market, labour is weak and workers have virtually no choice but to accept low wages and onerous contracts. We are told this is the way to get growth. Don't believe it. One of the reasons why Scotland and the UK's productivity is so poor is that employers, with subservient low-paid workers, have no reason to invest and workers no reason to contribute to productivity gains.

It is interesting that in pursuit of cuts, before the Budget in July, Tory MPs, along with some on the Left, were clamouring for an end to the bizarre situation that a company like Tesco, with pre-tax profits of £3.5

billion, can pay many of its workers low wages, which are then made up to a higher level by tax credits, paid by taxpayers. In Tesco's case this comes to £364 million a year. That is a subsidy to Tesco rather than the workers who are still on low income even with the credits. Tesco is not alone in feeding at the public trough in order to maintain low wages. ASDA gets £221 million, Sainsburys £181.5 million, Morrisons £189.5 million, Next £67.3 million. The total per year of low pay subsidy is £10.935 billion (Citizens UK).

This was something the Tory chancellor addressed in the actual Budget in July 2015, as part of a severe cuts policy. More on this later.

The permanent immigrant

We need young permanent immigrants in Scotland to boost the population, and bring new ideas and energy that will help us build sustainable growth. This category of migrant, like the temporary workers, will increase the numbers in the labour market, but the difference is that they will be the same as indigenous workers, having to run a home and clothe and feed their children, and so not so ready to be exploited on low wages. They will not only pay their taxes and national insurance, as do the temporary workers, but most of their money will be spent inside the Scottish economy, boosting demand. They will be more likely to look for trade union protection.

The traditional Scottish migrant countries, Australia, Canada and New Zealand, no longer operate an open-door policy, but one based on controlled numbers, with these judged on the contribution a migrant can make to the economy and society. They have differences in detail, but each seeks economic class migrants, which includes professionals, skilled workers and business class persons. Employer sponsorship is allowed for, and of course family sponsorship of a migrant. Australia decides on numbers admitted each year. Canada has a points system and age is a factor in that calculation. Happily there is no reference to skin colour in any of these programmes, although it is obvious that people from very poor countries with low educational levels have little chance of qualifying.

An independent Scotland would have to operate on a similar policy and models of implementation, if the purpose of our immigration policy is to grow the economy and fit migrants as easily as possible into our society.

As long as we remain a province within the UK, we control nothing. It is an evident benefit for the Scottish economy to enable those from abroad who qualify with a degree from our universities to stay here working for a period. This is a policy of the SNP. So far the UK government has not accepted it.

Thought, discussion, debate

In deciding to write about immigration I was aware that Enoch Powell with his rivers of blood speech, and UKIP with its scaremongering claim that all of Bulgaria can come here, have made immigration a toxic subject, with no-go areas and most people willing only to discuss it in private for fear of being branded racist.

We have to come out of the shadows those two created, and talk openly and honestly about how we develop policies on immigration that strike a balance between the needs of the Scottish economy, the views of indigenous Scots, the fact of continued migration, humanitarian demands, and rights of people who come here. It can be done, but only if there is open discussion based on the right to think and to put forward opinions, and debate.

Tory punishment for being a legal or illegal migrant worker

We in the UK and Scotland are going to have to face the fact of illegal immigrants living among us, just as the United States is having to do. I mentioned earlier the great character of those who start on a dangerous journey to get here, and that certainly applies to the illegals. Their tragedy, and it is a tragedy, is that they are wide open to exploitation by the worst elements in our society. They have no protection, and a future of no protection.

The Tories will, they say, make the money they earn, which will not be a lot, subject to the criminal law that allows proceeds of crime to be confiscated. This will not stop illegals staying, but it will make them even more vulnerable to exploitation by those who employ them. It is a kind of double jeopardy. This is taking scapegoating to a vicious level. Amnesty with right to remain here would be a more sensible policy.

The moves to restrict benefits to EU foreign workers will no doubt be popular, and sold on the basis that you cannot get certain benefits until you have been paying in. It may be popular in the abstract, but it will be difficult to sustain in terms of humanity when it comes to the individual. Are we really going to deny people a needed benefit, and make them and perhaps their families destitute? Has a good part of British society had its humanitarianism so bludgeoned with anti-immigrant propaganda that it would tolerate that?

That other national drink

Some may recall that day in Kilmarnock in July 2009, when political leaders, including the Tory Annabel Goldie, joined a mass demonstration of twenty thousand people against the decision by Diageo to close the Johnnie Walker plant in Kilmarnock, after 289 years, and the plant at Port Dundas in Glasgow. Nine hundred jobs went, seven hundred of them in Kilmarnock. The then local MP Des Browne, who doubled up as Scottish Secretary along with his defence job, rallied the march with these words aimed at Diageo, *"You seem to have forgotten that you don't own Jonnie Walker. The people of Kilmarnock do."* That of course was the problem. Neither in Kilmarnock or the rest of Scotland did, or do, the people own the Scottish whisky industry. Foreign companies own most of it. Brown's words went down well, but were empty of meaning.

When September came around, the twenty thousand might not have bothered marching. By then, Iain Gray, the Labour leader, was concerned about how the Scottish government might "mitigate" the effect on Kilmarnock, and Alex Salmond as First Minister had to sorrowfully record that the task force set up had "tried to reconcile Diageo's financial objectives of reducing costs and maximising profits with the social objectives of protecting communities at Port Dundas and Kilmarnock. To date the task force has not been successful." Nor could it be, because the one thing that could have saved the nine hundred jobs, a public stake in the industry, in a majority shareholding, was not on the cards and was not in any politician's mind.

Five years later, strangely, there was no great amount of attention given to the role of the whisky industry during the referendum although, like oil, it is one where the Scots cannot be threatened by taking it away on a vote for independence. That fact, when we come, hopefully to consider it next time, is something we should always bear in mind. Scotch whisky is here and cannot be produced anywhere else in the world.

It has been taken for granted that Scots gain from the whisky industry, and as each Westminster budget approaches pressure is on from its association and Scottish MPs to prevent any increase in duties. But we never seem to ask the question, what benefits do we really get from it?

Jobs? The Scotch Whisky Association states in its information package, that ten thousand jobs are directly involved in Scotland today, with over forty thousand jobs across the UK "supported" by the industry. There are 115 distilleries, with another thirty planned or being built. Whisky ownership is diverse, from family-run businesses to those classified as international. There have not been many in-depth studies of the industry. The latest I could find is by BIGGAR Economics, published in 2012, and one must work from that.

BIGGAR found that the distilleries are 83% foreign-owned. Distilleries do not employ large numbers of people. That leaves bottling, transport within the UK and transport to and from airports and docks for job creation. BIGGAR Economics estimated the industry turnover as £5.048 billion. Of this, £1.2 billion was for goods and services sourced in Scotland, and £0.536 million on employee costs. The operating profit was £3.013 billion. So, in jobs and supplies Scotland gained 35% of that turnover. The £3.03 billion profit mostly went out of the country.

In a recent publication, *Economic Policy Options for an Independent Scotland*, Professor John Kay is quoted: "I think the benefits to Scotland from the whisky industry are really quite disappointing. The largest producers are not based in Scotland. Their profits go mostly to people who are not resident in Scotland. They don't pay much tax in Scotland, and we don't think they pay much tax in the UK." The Scotch Whisky Association website claims the industry pays £1 billion each year in tax.

In their paper, *Economic Policy Options for an Independent Scotland*, the Cuthberts point out, "Figures quoted by industry insider Donnie Blair, in the *Sunday Herald* of 17 January 2010, showed that Scotch whisky volumes had been growing at what he described as an awesomely pedestrian rate of 0.082% per annum since 1978, while the equivalent growth rate for vodka over the last 20 years was 3.5%. Some industry insiders take the view that this has been the result of a deliberate policy ... as without the need for long periods locked up in bond, profit margins are higher for spirits like vodka."

Is that true? Is our indigenous industry being held back because the owners wish to give greater commercial emphasis to another product? The thing is we Scots don't know. As is always the case with an industry owned from outside, we have no real *knowledge* with which to judge. If the allegations are true, how are we to discuss sensibly issues affecting this industry, how it fits into the creation of a national tax base, and how we better employ it in our economy to create wealth and jobs that pay good wages?

Whisky is not, of course, the only key industry in foreign ownership. Our airports, important economic tools, are the same. Owners of Edinburgh, Glasgow and Aberdeen airports are also involved as investors in London's airports. It is from those southern airports that £2.4 billion of whisky is exported, compared to only £500 million from Scotland. That difference is not only a monetary one, but a jobs one as well.

Before the next referendum, Yes activists should be discussing this industry, and ways and means whereby Scots, who have no control now, exercise some degree of control in the future. One way suggested by the Options paper is to alter the licence arrangements. Another is public participation in ownership of the large companies.

The role of public power in a mixed economy

Public power will be exercised through legislation enacted in the independent parliament at Holyrood, as constrained by a written constitution. For those on the Left, the question is where to direct that power so as to alter the economic structure of the country, to make its people wealthier and end poverty. There is a matter of principle here: in economic structures the public interest must take preference over the interests of other economic actors. That is a principle, not a dogma. It has to be applied with common sense, not ideological fervour. The socialist movement should have enough gumption, if not humility, to acknowledge that in parts of the world where its ideology has been applied against common sense, in agriculture and the small business sectors in the USSR and Mao's China, it brought failure on a grand scale.

That principle allied to common sense has to be applied in a mixed economy with small businesses, larger national ones, and multinational ones operating and contributing to GDP, with Scotland linked into a global economy. The principle is perhaps best employed in those economic areas that are fundamental to the lives of the citizens – the utilities that are needed by all, such as electricity and gas, NHS, plus those essential to the economy, like rail and bus services, and where our natural resources are not run in the national interest. The best way to exercise public power over our natural resources and in the utilities is to take them into public ownership, but that might not be possible in terms of 100% ownership, as there can be no expropriation. But public power involvement there has to be.

There is also the use of public power in assisting business to develop and enter into new markets in the growing Asian region. Of particular importance is the small and medium-sized business sector (SMEs) which, as I wrote in *In Place of Fear II*, represents local capital that poses no threat to the communities in which it is born and works. That sector has real potential for growth and job creation, and is a legitimate area for government assistance in research, development and help in breaking into foreign markets. Public policy also has a role in encouraging science and advanced engineering excellence.

The point is that the Left, before independence and as preparation for it, should start thinking outside the mental box that imprisons us in the UK. The Jimmy Reid Foundation and Common Weal are doing that, and there are signs that others are doing the same.

Tackling inequality

Absolute equality of income is not possible, but differences in income in a decent society need not matter provided the gap between those paid most and those paid least is not excessively large. When that gap widens, and continues to widen, leaving a huge gulf between a small elite and the rest, with those at the very bottom mired in poverty, then we are into the issue of gross inequality, which is the case in the UK and Scotland today.

That is unhealthy for a society, because it indicates a lack of morality on the part of those who most influence and control wealth distribution, and undermines the solidarity and mutual concern that is the social glue that holds a nation together.

At the heart of this is the distribution of wealth. People get or earn their share of wealth in a variety of ways. It can be from salary for work undertaken, dividends in shares, exploiting shortages in land or housing, profits from commercial activities, welfare benefits, or the state and private pensions. These are but some of the ways.

There are some on the Right who claim that objections to extreme wealth, with a small group getting most, is the politics of envy, which they also claim is the hallmark of socialism. This is where they err. There is a general recognition among people that there is an imbalance of power in our society, and the way power is distributed now is damaging to many thousands of human beings.

The result of gross inequality is high levels of poverty. Poverty crushes people, and communities disintegrate under its pressure. Children in particular suffer. Extensive research has shown that a child conceived in poverty is handicapped from the womb, and in its first three years after birth. It will always lag behind its peer group in the rest of society. Of course there will be those gifted with such talent that they escape, but that does not apply to the majority.

Taking action
The private sector

Before setting out the action that can be taken, some background to company law is required, because it is here in the private sector that a remedy exists to constrain the inequalities in the distribution of incomes. The public sector presents other ways to curb excessive differences in income.

A plc, a public limited company, differs in no way from a limited liability company, in that both have a considerable advantage over any other type of company – if they go bottom up the shareholders are not liable personally for any debts incurred by the company.

Limited liability is a nineteenth-century legal description of a company. Its removal of huge personal risk enabled capital to invest where risk was involved, and without it the Industrial Revolution would have advanced at a much slower pace. Limited liability is the gift of public law. It is a gift that can be withdrawn, but which would be catastrophic for the investment communities, so that is not available. We have to look at other options.

As it is public law it can be amended. Nothing stops a sovereign government from amending the limited liability law to make it contingent on conditions about salary and benefits differentials for those who work for the company, say, laying down in law the differences in what the board, senior managers and employees earn.

At present these differentials are out of hand. It is reckoned between when the banks were responsible institutions up to the 1990s, before the casino era that brought about the crash, that the top people got no more than twenty times what the lowest paid got. Now it can be four hundred times more or higher. Sir Terry Leahy was paid almost nine hundred times more than the average worker in Tesco (*The New Few*, by Ferdinand Mount).

We need a radical policy that imposes a legal obligation on plcs and other limited liability companies in return for continued protection. Let us say paying the top managers and board no more than twenty-five times what the lowest paid worker earns. This need for a better ratio of top to bottom pay is not only promoted by someone on the left. In *The New Few*, Mount quoted Sir Stuart Rose, former CEO of Marks & Spencer, endorsing the Hutton Report on fair pay back in 2011: "There's no doubt about it, we have to accept that over the last year or three the division between the lowest paid and the highest has got wider, so that does need looking at" (p. 204).

Mount, no Leftie he, has punted the idea of a code of "stewardship" that would require the ratio in a medium-sized company to be 20-1, in a large company 40-1, with no cash bonus to exceed 20% of salary. Stewardship is a nice notion, but I prefer the rigour of the law. That way it will happen. A phase-in of five years should suffice.

That will bring cries of distress from boardrooms, telling us we are putting up barriers to recruiting the best talent. Really? The facts don't bear that claim out. The "best talent" they have recruited have been far from good managers of some of the largest and previously most successful companies, and have either brought them to their knees or cast them into oblivion.

We all know about the bank failures where personal fortunes were paid to get that talent, but there are other commercial fields in which the claim of buying the best is, shall we say, doubtful. The supermarkets are a case in point, but there are many others. One that has received little attention is the fate of GEC, one of the largest manufacturing and technological companies in Europe when the new expensive management took over. In addition to a successful company, they inherited £5 billion cash in the bank. In a short space of time all that cash had gone, and the company in its final demise saw the share price go from £12.50 to 6p.

Taking action
The public sector

Tackling inequality of income can be exercised reasonably quickly in the public sector. The main paymasters are either central government and its agencies, or the local authorities. Again, given that contracts will be in place, it is necessary to phase in a policy.

Over a five-year period the ratio between the highest and lowest paid in any public service organisation should be 20-1, reducing over the next five years to 13-1. The practice of paying very senior people, already on high salaries, a bonus for doing what they are paid for can come to an end. Such a policy would reintroduce what Ferdinand Mount might think of as the responsibility of stewardship; in my book it is the reintroduction of the concept of public service.

Taking action
On the wage front and Tory policy

Introducing new policies on ratios in both private and public sectors is more than symbolic, and will have a profound effect about how society develops its sense of mutual responsibility, but it does not answer the question of how to end gross inequality in the distribution of income. *That can only be done by raising substantially the wages of the lower paid.*

How important that simple fact is can be borne out by looking at the situation. Poverty Alliance research has shown that 18% of the Scottish workforce earn less than the living wage, 64% of low-wage workers are women, 40% are women working part-time, and 93% of low paid are in the private sector, with hospitality and retail sectors particularly bad payers.

As mentioned previously, reducing the Tesco subsidy through cutting tax credits was a pre-Budget campaign. In his July 2015 Budget statement the chancellor cut the tax credits and, repeating himself to make sure we all got it, triumphantly announced he was introducing a compulsory new national living wage, which would reach £9 an hour by 2020, five years away. The problem with budget speeches is that they are for political effect, replete with sound bites designed for the next day's newspaper headlines, while the detail is left unexplored until the analysts have studied the Red Book and the volume of other information that comes when the Minister sits down.

Within an hour of him sitting down, it became clear that he would not be the one to determine the pace of progress from next April's figure, towards the £9 in 2020. It would be passed to the Low Pay Commission to set the phased increases. Also the new living wage would only be compulsory for people aged twenty-five and over. So, the minimum wage for the young remains. Osborne never mentioned that. Nor did he provide, in his speech, any examples of how the combination of cuts to tax credits and the living wage would affect family incomes.

As is usual with a budget, once the Red Book and other documents have been examined, the reality is different from the message presented in the chancellor's speech. The tax credit system, of which the Tesco subsidy is part, has become so labyrinthine, and the family circumstances of those affected by the cuts he introduced so varied, that it will take a long time for us to know what the Budget really means.

Any idea that ipso facto the Tescos of this world will make up in wages what is lost in tax credits is to believe in the tooth fairy.

Will the national living wage really raise incomes?

That, therefore, begs the question of whether the new living wage will really raise incomes, because the low paid are not disentangled from the tax credit system, with some post-Budget assessments showing that many will have lower net incomes.

People employed by the 1,000 companies paying the living wage in 2015 received £7.85 an hour – £9.15 in London. Will a rise of £1.15 between now and 2020 catapult them into a higher standard of living? Hardly.

But what of the minimum wage earners? The minimum wage for the 25+ age group will, from October 2015, be £6.70. In April 2016, with the living wage introduced it will become £7.20. By 2020 that will be an increase phased in, of £1.80. What about the young? They are stuck on the minimum wage, with the 20-24 age group denied the living wage. Considering that a large number of those on the minimum wage are part-time, it is little wonder that inequality has been growing apace.

The principle of a national living wage, higher in value than a minimum wage, is a good one. The test, however, is whether the rate set, the age ranges it applies to, and its relation to inflation over time, is really at a level at which people can pay their bills, feed their children properly, and escape the permanent financial insecurity that plagues millions. An eventual, step-by-step rise, from £7.85 to £9 does not meet that need.

The inescapable fact is that there is no possibility of improved equality, through incomes, if our society remains anchored in low pay, due to two factors: high unemployment which forces people to sell their labour cheaply, and its concomitant, that employers, including SMEs, are under no pressure to raise the level of investment and innovate because labour is cheap. Just what low pay means was highlighted by The Herald (9 July 2015): noting the Budget tax trigger for income tax now rises from 10,600 to 11,000 a year, it commented that this "will take thousands of Scots out of paying income tax." Thousands on less than half the average wage!

I watched, following the Budget speech, the media interviewing employers in the SME sector, all of whom pleaded an inability to match the new living wage levels. I have a great regard for the people who run small businesses, knowing the personal risk and effort they make to start up and get through the early difficult years. I have argued *In Place of Fear II* that they should be assisted by a special small business investment bank.

But the level of examination of this sector is superficial. None of those interviewed were asked about their income level, or their level of profit. None were asked if they could not raise their prices to pay a living wage. The answer, of course, would be that would put them out of business as competitors would not do the same. *That can be overcome by legislation creating a level playing field.*

Use the law where it can be effective on wage levels

Neither in the UK or anywhere else is there a free market. Public law has long been needed, and employed, to prevent abuse of economic power or irresponsible conduct by companies. In our financial sector we have the Bank of England as a regulator, along with other instruments such as the Financial Conduct Authority which regulates over fifty thousand businesses. We also have a history of wage regulation in the agricultural sector.

So, there would be nothing new in principle or practice, for a new law making it compulsory to pay the living wage for anyone over twenty years of age, in the retail and service sectors. That would prevent one employer undercutting another through low wages, and it would have a beneficial effect for workers in the retail and hospitality sectors which are notorious for consistent low pay. That could mean a rise in prices in some subsections of those sectors, but a society that says it is willing to pay fair trade prices for imported products, so that people are not exploited in developing countries, can hardly complain at legislation aimed at fair wages to remove exploitation in their own country.

The only way to make a real difference now

To really start making a difference, the living wage would have to rise *next year* to £10 and £11 from 2017. I know the arguments for a lower rate of minimum wage for young people, that it enables them to get a foot on the employment ladder, because otherwise employers would not take them on at a higher rate of pay. I don't buy it entirely. I can see that argument for a youngster just leaving school, who has yet to gain experience, but not for someone aged twenty and over. They may be young adults, but they are adults. The fact is that the age group 16-24 present, now a pool of talented cheap labour, leaving employers no incentive to improve their business in order to attract them at a reasonable rate of pay.

One of the problems with the UK economy, and that includes Scotland, is that productivity is poor. In France, employee costs per worker are some 30-40% higher than the UK. That higher labour cost has forced employers, in order to remain competitive within and outwith the EU, to invest, because it is investment in new and up-to-date equipment and machinery that determines productivity. Our low wage economy, with employers subsidised by government to the tune of almost £11 billion a year (according to Citizens UK's research), is a barrier to investment.

Not only on the issue of morality, but from the point of view of stimulating growth through productivity instead of debt, replacing the minimum wage with the living wage for all from twenty years and over, is sensible. What cannot be allowed to happen to the living wage is what happened to the minimum wage – the erosion of its value.

Conclusion

It may be that some of the ideas I have advanced in my first referendum book *In Place of Fear II*, and in this one, will come to nothing. However, I am reminded of advice from an old Labour Party member when I first joined in 1960. He said that ideas in politics were like the seed a farmer scattered on the ground some took root and grew, while others lay fallow, only to come good in later times, and that there was no reason to explain this.

I can confirm that this is so. In a House of Commons debate, 3 May 1972, during the passage of the bill for entry into the EEC, I made a speech which reflected my move from staunch Unionist to a devolutionist teetering on the brink of independence. The Labour Party had trounced the SNP in local elections the day before, so I felt able to speak without being accused of panic in the face of a nationalist advance.

I forecast as a result of EEC entry "acute problems for all the people of the United Kingdom" holding the Union together, something that might take "10 or 15 years to manifest itself" and went on to argue "if the European Communities pursue the Werner plan for economic and monetary union, the logic which brings us to Westminster may take us to Brussels, because certain Scottish interests which would be termed regional interests in the context of the United Kingdom would be converted to distinct national interests if Scotland were represented in Brussels." That was the first time the idea was aired of Scotland being a separate member state in the European Union, albeit clothed in a question rather than a bold assertion. No one listening agreed with me, and some could not grasp what I was talking about. It was a late night speech, 10.45 p.m., so there was no mention in the newspapers next day.

Three years later, once again having travelled along

a difficult political road, within a few days of the 1975 referendum result on remaining in the EEC, I produced and presented a paper at a press conference where I did assert the need for a Scottish separate state to be represented in Brussels. The journalists attending were puzzled, and could not understand what I was getting at. In 1988, at another press conference, I set out "Independence in Europe" for the SNP. The journalists, some of whom attended the one in 1975, thought it a new, great idea. Now, Scotland as a member of the EU is part and parcel of orthodox thinking. Ideas, like seeds, can grow when the political soil is ready.

I hope some of the seeds that I have planted in my previous book and this one, will take root and grow some day.

Acknowledgements

A number of people have been extremely helpful, providing information, guiding me towards research, engaging in discussion, criticising. I would in particular like to thank Peter Kearney, Calum Miller, Professor Joe Farrell and Allan Cameron (the publisher) for the support they have given, and for all they have done to make this book possible.

Dr. Jim Walker of the Austrian school of economics, who has been a friend of mine and Margo's for many years and who, despite our different positions on the ideological spectrum, has been unstinting in his provision of information, advice and criticism, as have Jim and Margaret Cuthbert whose international standard research has been a joy to mine. Nick Dekker I am indebted to for the knowledge he so readily passed on about the oil industry and energy policy.

I could not pass without thanking Alex Neil MSP, not for his input of comments on this book which he could not do as a government minister, but for the years of our comradeship during which our conversations have roamed over national, international and ideological subjects, and from which I learned much.

The views set out in this book are, of course, my own.